THE GREAT BOOK OF DOGS

An International Anthology

By Gino Pugnetti

**Paintings and Drawings
by Piero Cozzaglio**

THE GREAT BOOK OF DOGS

An International Anthology

By Gino Pugnetti

Paintings and Drawings by Piero Cozzaglio

Galahad Books
A Division of A & W Publishers
New York

Contents

Introduction

For centuries men and women the world over have depended on dogs—as their partners in work and play, as the guardians of their homes, families and flocks, and, simply, as loving, loyal companions. Throughout history we have bred and adapted dogs to fulfill our every need, until today dogs come in every size, color, and shape—with personalities to fit every circumstance.

Never before has there been such intense and widespread interest in purebred dogs. Each year more and more people attend dog shows, more and more dogs are shown, and more and more families choose pedigreed dogs for pets. This is due, in part, to increased leisure time and interest in dogs as a specialized hobby—but even more to the growing realization that for purely practical and humanitarian reasons dog owners should know as much as they possibly can about their pets. No pet should be acquired frivolously, only to be given away or abandoned when it does not fit into the family way of life. There is a dog to suit every purpose and every life-style, if only dog owners will take the time to learn about them.

While the tradition of the family mutt is as American as Thanksgiving turkey and fire crackers on the Fourth of July, realistically, the mongrel is always an unknown quantity. That cute, cuddly puppy with the huge paws and the velvet muzzle, may grow up to be the menace of the neighborhood, an embarrassment to the whole family, but a dog of a recognized breed from a dependable kennel can be counted on to exhibit certain predetermined characteristics. The apartment dweller who knows about dogs can select a pet small enough to share restricted quarters comfortably, with the low energy level that requires only brief daily walks. Informed parents can choose a loyal, loving, and playful companion for their children, or, if safety is an important factor, a watchful guard dog. The hunter can choose a breed that is intelligent, disciplined, and uniquely adapted to his preferred sport. But first they must know.

THE GREAT BOOK OF DOGS describes more than 300 different breeds of dogs and tells the fascinating story of their evolution and their long association with man. In these pages you will meet 24 different breeds of terriers, each developed at a different time and place to meet a specific need: the Bedlington Terrier, bred by the miners of the English town of Bedlington to combat the rats in their mines; the Border Terrier from the frontier between England and Scotland, a small dog with a flat otterlike head uniquely adapted to combatting the bloodthirsty local foxes; the Cairn Terrier, developed to rout out the wild animals that hid in Scotland's stone grave-markers (cairns); and the Dandy Dinmont, a droll dog with the look of a melancholy clown, named after a character in Sir Walter Scott's novel, *Guy Mannering*. The hunter, traditionally the most informed of dog owners, will find no less than 99 distinctive hunting dogs: spaniels, terriers, dachshunds, retrievers, pointers, and hounds. There are chapters on sheepdogs, bouviers, watchdogs, guard dogs, rescue dogs, sled dogs, hunting dogs, and companion dogs. There are dogs from England, Scotland, Wales, Hungary, France, Belgium, Sweden, Yugoslavia, Germany, Mexico ... dogs introduced into Italy by the Phoenicians, dogs represented on ancient Greek coins and in Egyptian sculpture, dogs developed in 19th-century Europe, and dogs that only received recognition yesterday ... dogs that were the companions of kings and queens, and dogs that have worked for centuries alongside of the shepherd ... dogs with flat paws adapted to walking over deep snow, and dogs with a special instinct for pulling things out of the water ... loyal, friendly, funny dogs—proud, haughty dogs.

Gifted Italian artist Piero Cozzaglio has captured in paintings and drawings the distinctive qualities of each breed as no photographs possibly could.

Sheepdogs

Longhaired
German Shepherd

11   It is said that around the year 1000 a group of Scottish monks wishing to defend their monastery against marauders created a new, strong, and bold watchdog by crossing local sheepdogs with wolves. The monks obtained a majestic animal, intelligent, courageous, and aggressive, but easy to train: the first German Shepherd. Perhaps this genesis is steeped in legend, but the dog we know and admire today under the name German Shepherd was first presented officially at the Stuttgart Dog Show of 1887, and it was truly the result of a cross between sheepdogs and wolves. From this time on, this magnificent dog, veritable king of the canine world, was officially named the German Shepherd, though it was commonly but erroneously called "Wolf-Dog."

  Unlike other breeds, the German Shepherd has not suffered over the years from the caprice of fashion. There have always been numerous dog lovers in the world who have kept Shepherds, with a loyalty equal to that shown by the dog itself. It is impossible to count the number of human lives saved during the two world wars by German Shepherds. They instinctively found the wounded and bore them to safety, transported medicines and messages under artillery fire, sounded alarms, and located people buried under the debris of bombardments. More recently, their help has been indispensable after earthquakes and avalanches. And, finally, one cannot forget the role of German Shepherd as police dog, popularized in movies and television in the character of Rin Tin Tin.

  Handsome and imposing of bearing, happy, alert, extremely vigilant, honest, daring, ideal as a watchdog and bodyguard: all these qualities are an essential part of the German Shepherd. A dog of this breed would be considered just as imperfect if he were apathetic or overexcitable as he would if he had such physical defects as a short muzzle, jaws which did not meet properly, bow legs, or defective balance.

  It is wrong to say that the German Shepherd is not suitable for apartment life. It is only necessary to exercise him frequently in order to keep him in good shape. What the German Shepherd needs most is an energetic master who can dominate him and make him obey. Training in a specialized school is also essential so that the dog will learn to obey commands as soon as they are given. There is a saying: "The German Shepherd is either at your feet or at your throat." Nothing is truer. He will be at the feet of his master and his friends, of the wounded and the blind, ready to obey and bring help; but he will be at the throat of the wrongdoer.

  The ideal height for the German Shepherd is 24 to 26 inches (61 to 66 cm.) for the male and 22 to 24 inches (56 to 61 cm.) for bitches. He must never be clipped, because the sun on his skin is not healthy for him. In the summer, he requires a good brushing and a bath from time to time.

German Shepherd

**Shorthaired
German Shepherd**

12 Toward the end of the nineteenth century, Belgian dog lovers noticed that the quality of the sheepdogs was degenerating and that they sometimes showed signs of viciousness. With the support of the university faculty of veterinary science, specialists decided to stabilize definitively the breed of Belgian Sheepdog. The dog breeder Nicholas Rose played a very important part in this long and delicate undertaking. In one of his sheepdog litters, Monsieur Rose found an all-black bitch with long hair. At the end of the nineteenth century, black was an unusual color for a dog's coat, and it was therefore decided to search out an identical male. A year later, the little bitch, Petite, had a mate, Piccard. In 1898, the couple bore a litter of all-black puppies which became the sensation of the dog world. Because of the success of the new Belgian Sheepdog, dog lovers wanted to give the breed the name of its developer: Rose. Rose, however, was obviously not the right name for an all-black dog; so, since Monsieur Rose was the owner of Groenendael castle on the outskirts of Brussels, it was decided that Groenendael should be the official name of the Belgian Sheepdog.

Intelligent and easy to train, his usefulness is comparable to that of the German Shepherd, and he has given great service in both war and peacetime. He is as good a watchdog as he is a shepherd, and he is still incomparable at guarding the flocks. Today, the Groenendael, true cousin to the German Shepherd, is enjoying considerable popularity in Europe and America. He is distinguished by his lively intelligence, his courage, his friendliness toward children, and his remarkable aptitude as a watchdog and bodyguard. At the same time, it is highly recommended that anyone wishing to own a Belgian Sheepdog have it trained by a professional trainer, who can, in a matter of a few months, curb any potentially aggressive behavior.

Belgian Sheepdog (Groenendael)

Longhaired
Belgian Shepherd
(Groenendael)

13   The Belgian Sheepdog is an elegant dog with a thick, shiny black coat. His height at the withers should be 24 to 26 inches (61 to 66 cm.), with females measuring from 22 to 24 inches (56 to 61 cm.). Suspicious of strangers and other dogs, he shows boundless affection for his master. By nature, he needs to be exercised over long distances. His coat needs washing from time to time and frequent brushing, but clipping is not advised.

The Groenendael has two close relatives who differ from him only in the color of their coats. The Tervuren has long hair of a warm fawn color and sometimes a black mask. The Malinois has short, fawn-colored hair with charcoal or gray markings and a black mask. Today, these are each recognized as separate breeds in the United States.

Longhaired Belgian Shepherd (Tervuren)

Shorthaired Belgian Shepherd (Malinois)

Like all sheepdogs, the Berger de Beauce, or Beauceron, has very ancient origins. There was a time when he was a dangerous and savage-looking animal. Today his character has improved, but he has kept the physical qualities of former times: height around 28 inches (71 cm.) and weight around 66 pounds (30 kg.). He is a muscular, rustic, wolflike dog. In France he is still known by the nickname "Red Stockings" because of his unusual coloration: dark liver with fiery red patches on his feet and thighs.

The Beauceron was originally only a sheepdog, but his intelligence, the ease with which he can be trained, and his powerful bite have promoted him to the ranks of police dog and bodyguard. His only disadvantage is his extreme aggressiveness toward strangers.

Beauceron

15 The Briard, or Berger de Brie, a very old breed, is the most popular and important sheepdog in France. In appearance it resembles the Bergamasco, the Komondor, and the Bearded Collie: all sheepdogs which clearly share a common ancestry. The breed probably originated in the Orient, but before the year 1000 it was at home in France. It is known that Charlemagne bred Briards and that the breed gradually spread from the province of Brie over the whole of France. Its appearance changed scarcely at all through the centuries, and it received official recognition as a breed in the Parisian Exposition of 1886.

   The Briard is a born country dog, a sensible farm dog, as rustic of coat as of personality, with its long hair as rough as the hair of a goat, its beard, moustache, and bushy eyebrows complementing a gruff but kindly personality. Although originally a sheepdog, the Briard has, over time, proved its aptitude as a guard dog and a companion. During the First World War, the breed distinguished itself. Because of its extremely sensitive hearing, it was used by the French to warn their sentries of danger. What was really astounding, however, was its instinct not only for finding the wounded but for reliably pointing out the most serious cases first.

   Sturdy and well-proportioned, the Briard is an agile, muscular dog. The male should measure between 23 and 27 inches (58,5 to 68,5 cm.), the female between 22 and 25½ inches (56 to 65 cm.). The Briard should never be bathed or clipped, only curried with a hard brush, one with metal bristles perhaps, which will remove all the loose hair from its bushy head to its long, hooked tail.

   In recent years the Briard has gained new popularity, especially in America where he is appreciated for his intelligence, his rough dignity, and his gentle, wide-eyed expression which can be glimpsed every now and then through the tangled hair of his face. All solid colors are allowed except white.

Briard

16   Cousin to the Briard, the Pyrenees Sheepdog is a lively animal with thick, goatlike hair and expressive eyes. He is a true son of the Pyrenees. The breed has evolved there naturally over the centuries, without any crossbreeding. Because he has developed in the harsh climate of the mountains, accustomed to hard work over rocky ground, this sheepdog is perhaps the most resistant of all dogs, not only to bad weather conditions, but also to viral infections such as distemper and hepatitis.

    This sturdy, bold, and agile little dog is so daring and strong that he will not hesitate to attack a wolf or even a bear. Although moody with strangers, he is extremely devoted to his master to whom he is a loyal and affectionate companion. Indeed, the alacrity with which he anticipates his master's wishes is astounding. His coat may be tawny, silver gray, or white with yellowish patches. Height: 20 inches (50 cm.). Weight: from 44 to 52 pounds (20 to 24 kg.).

Pyrenees Sheepdog

17 The two breeds of Pyrenees Sheepdog are distinguished from one another not only by their size, but by their hairstyles. While the smaller Pyrenees Sheepdog is shaggy from head to tail, the Smooth-Muzzled Pyrenees Sheepdog has shorter hair, especially on his head. His muzzle is also somewhat longer. The hair on his front legs is extremely short while that on his hind legs grows to form a ''pair of breeches.''

An altogether loveable dog, the Smooth-Muzzled Pyrenees Sheepdog is calm by nature, but will immediately chase away anyone who dares to approach his flock. His eyes are expressive and somewhat melancholy looking. Docile and with good reflexes, he is readily trainable as a watchdog or bodyguard. His average height is 26 inches (65 cm.); his weight, 110 pounds (50 kg.). His coat is most commonly tawny red, harlequined black, or mottled gray with or without white flecking. Less common are uniformly gray individuals.

Smooth-Muzzled Pyrenees Sheepdog

Another French sheepdog, the Picardy Sheepdog, is one of the oldest breeds of shepherd, and its origins are obscure. Fairly popular, especially in the north of France, he is a dog with very thick, rough hair, a true farmyard dog who has only recently received official recognition. In appearance, he resembles the Griffon. He is an outstanding herder of sheep and an excellent farm guard, alert and vigilant, but never aggressive toward strangers.

He has a beard and moustache, but they do not succeed in making him look harsh. As usual, the male is taller and heavier than the female: 24 to 26 inches (61 to 65 cm.) versus 22 to 24 inches (56 to 61 cm.). The coat is rough, of average length, and may be gray, slate gray, blue gray, or various shades of tan.

Picardy Sheepdog

19 The Hungarian nomads who have bred the Komondor for thousands of years have given him the title "King of the Working Dogs." With his rough, shaggy, often dirty coat, so long that it drags on the ground, the Komondor is anything but an aristocrat. But much toil, much devotion, and many bitter struggles have marked his long history on the steppes of Hungary. He will lie quietly, watching the flocks with his dreamy expression and leaving the petty task of surveillance to dogs of lesser breed. But at the first hint of danger, the Komondor rises to his full, imposing height (it often exceeds 31 inches (78,7 cm.)), and in his veins surges the blood of the wolf, with which, centuries ago, shepherds bred his forefathers. These forefathers, in turn, were brought from the East by Magyar nomads. A majestic, snarling dog, the Komondor will not hesitate to confront ferociously anything which disturbs the peace of the flock, even a wolf or a bear, and if provoked, he is ready to fight to the death. Only the intervention of his master can calm his overwhelming anger.

His tough, woolly coat becomes as impermeable as felt on his paws and abdomen and protects him both from the biting cold winds of the plains and from the fangs of predators. The Komondor, with his thick coat and sharp teeth, rarely emerges from battle beaten and bloody. The Hungarian police have trained several of these dogs as city police dogs, and the results have been excellent, especially when it has come to chasing a fleeing criminal.

The true color of the Komondor's coat is pure white, but this is only seen at dog shows, where he is presented after several baths. In the Hungarian steppes, with only the rain to wash him, he is, at best, gray.

Komondor

In general appearance the Puli resembles the Komondor, but he is smaller and his coat is dark. Furthermore, while the Komondor is equally suited to guarding the block or the house, the more dynamic Puli, or Hungarian Sheepdog, is, above all, a specialist in herding sheep. He is a fine sight, moving ceaselessly, maneuvering around and among the flock, jumping at the necks of rams and ewes. If he is well trained, his swiftness is without equal. In the eighteenth century, he was also used for hunting in marshy areas with excellent results. His woolly coat, which tends to curl and mat, protected him from the wet.

   Although suspicious toward strangers, the Puli is lively and bold and makes a delightful companion. Average height in dogs is 17 inches (43 cm.) and must not exceed 19 inches (48,3 cm.). Bitches average 16 inches (40,6 cm) and must not exceed 18 inches (45,7 cm.).

   A breed very like the Puli, the Pumi, has a thinner coat and is slightly taller. More high-spirited, he has a characteristic springy gait and is in many ways similar to the terrier.

Puli

21 For centuries, this huge, brave dog was in the service of the Hungarian nobility. During the fifteenth century, a period marked by political and military unrest, King Mathias I put more trust in his Kouvaszes than in his ambitious courtiers. When the king died in 1490, the Kouvasz had to adapt itself to a new life as a guard dog on the farm and a sheepdog on the steppes. Vigilant and majestic in his white coat, he was always ready to confront wolves on equal terms and to pursue and catch the wily fox.

The name Kouvasz derives from the Turkish word *kawsz* (trusty guard), which seems to indicate that the breed was brought to Hungary thousands of years ago by nomadic Turkish shepherds at the same time as the Puli and the Komondor, though he may have accompanied the invading Huns. Today, the regal Kouvasz, while still a sheepdog and guard dog, is mainly known as a luxury dog. He is a faithful house dog and an ideal companion for children. He measures between 28 and 30 inches (71 to 76 cm.) in height. Bitches may be somewhat smaller.

Kouvasz

22   His coat is sometimes so shaggy and bushy that it is difficult to make out the shape of the dog. Although one would immediately categorize him as a sheepdog, an outside dog, the Bergamasco's temperament is such that he adapts equally well to apartment life or to the role of watchdog or bodyguard. Firemen in various countries often use him to seek out the wounded.

The geneology of the Bergamasco goes back two thousand years when the Phoenicians introduced him into Europe. Settled briefly in Tuscany, the Bergamasco was progenitor of the Maremma Sheepdog. The breed then established itself in the North of Italy, probably in the vicinity of Bergamo from which it took its name. Finally, it spread to France and England where, without doubt, it contributed to the development of the Briard and the Bobtail.

The average height of the Bergamasco is around 24 inches (61 cm.). He weighs between 66 and 88 pounds (30 to 40 kg.). He has a solid, sturdy body covered with long, rough, wavy hair in all shades of gray. His eyes are dark and have a sweet expression. His naturally short tail is slightly curved at the end and is carried low in repose and high in motion.

Unfortunately, it is difficult today to find an absolutely purebred Bergamasco. Foregoing serious breeding and valuing usefulness over any aesthetic considerations, shepherds and farmers have taken hardly any precautions when it comes to breeding the Bergamasco. This is a serious mistake, because experience has shown that in a carefully developed, pure breed, physical excellence is always accompanied by mental excellence. This is particularly true of the Bergamasco, which possesses a high degree of intelligence, a capacity for observation, and a remarkable memory. He is easy to train and is courageous, sweet, and calm.

Bergamasco

23 This is the most beautiful of the sheepdogs. Imposing, intelligent, good-hearted, and strong, this breed has been, since ancient times, the indispensable companion of the shepherds of Abruzzi, Maremma, and the Roman countryside. From the days of the Roman Empire, white sheepdogs were preferred, because they were easy to distinguish from wild animals, and one could run to them confidently when in need of help.

For a long time, the two varieties of this breed—the Abruzzi and the Maremma—were confused with one another. Although the Abruzzi may be a little smaller, it is now common to speak of them as a single breed.

The Maremma is an exceptionally big dog: height, 28 inches (71 cm); weight, 100 pounds (45 kg.). He has long, harsh hair which is shorter on the head. His coat should be uniformly white, although ivory and slight traces of yellow are allowed. He has a large head, dark, trusting eyes, triangular pendent ears, and sharp teeth. Majestic under his rustic exterior, the Maremma is hardy, lively, and intelligent. He is an incomparable sheepdog, but also an excellent, even ferocious, guardian of the country home.

The breed was only recognized in Italy in 1915, twenty centuries after it first appeared in Abruzzi. Even after that, few breeders succeeded in finding combinations which preserved all the aesthetic qualities and working abilities required by the Standard. English dog lovers, however, applied themselves to the problem. Having acquired several prized individuals, they succeeded in developing the breed and exporting Maremmas throughout the world, including to Italy, their native country. The Maremma is not an apartment dog. He needs an outside exercise area and someplace where he can escape from the sun, since shearing is inadvisable.

Maremma Sheepdog (Abruzzi Sheepdog)

24 The Swedish Shepherd, or Västgötaspets, has physical and working characteristics very similar to those of the Corgi, but Swedish dog lovers insist that he is of strictly national origin and breeding and is related neither closely nor distantly to similar dogs of other provenance.

Like the Corgi, the Swedish Shepherd is a little dog with naturally likeable looks. He has an elongated body, short legs, and lively, dark, almond-shaped eyes. Strong and eager, he is an outstanding guard and an excellent herder, able to withstand whole nights out in the cold and to run around for hours on end during the day.

His coat is harsh and thick, grayish in color with a long darker band down the back. He has a short tail that must not measure more than four inches (10 cm.) according to the official Standard and which he holds erect when he is about to embark on some bold enterprise. He measures from 12 to 13 inches (30,5 to 33 cm.) at the shoulder and weighs 20 to 31 pounds (9,1 to 14,2 kg.).

Recently, Swedish Shepherds have been brought into town as companion dogs, but they seem to have difficulty adapting to the new conditions and are frequently subject to nervousness.

Swedish Shepherd (Västgötaspets)

25 Bearing a certain resemblance to the Collie, but with a larger, squarer head, the Sar Planina is the most common sheepdog in Yugoslavia. He is especially popular on the Adriatic side of the peninsula in the region which in ancient Roman times was called Illyria and from which he takes his name. His origins, like those of all sheepdogs, are probably Eastern. The present Illyrian Sheepdog, the result of local matings and long acclimatization, was recognized as an indigenous breed and given a Standard in 1930.

He is a difficult dog, distrustful of strangers, and usually obedient to only one master. Like all shepherds who live in inaccessible areas, his number-one enemy is the wolf.

The Yugoslavian Standard establishes his height as $21\frac{1}{2}$ to $23\frac{1}{2}$ inches (54,6 to 60 cm.) and his weight as between 66 and 77 pounds (30 to 35 kg.), a little less for bitches. He has a long (about 4 inches (10 cm.)), thick coat which is gray and, sometimes, has a black mask.

Illyrian Sheepdog (Sar Planina)

26 Sturdy, strong, and bold, the Karst is the ideal dog for harsh terrain, rocky mountains, and cutting winds. Although he lives almost exclusively in Yugoslavia, the Karst is worthy of mention as a thoughtful guardian of proven loyalty and dignified bearing. He is a good-natured dog, but he will not tolerate any disrespect toward his master.

The Karst is from 21½ to 23½ inches tall (54,6 to 60 cm.) and weighs from 66 to 88 pounds (30 to 40 kg.). He has a gray coat similar to the wolf's. He has almond-shaped eyes, laid-back ears, and round, solid feet made to cope with rocky ground. In addition to being useful with the flocks, he is a delightful companion dog. The Yugoslavian shepherds are well aware of this, as they spend long months with their dogs, in harmony and security far from civilization.

Another Yugoslavian dog with a noteworthy instinct for watching over the flocks is the Croatian Sheepdog.

Karst

27   A thick shaggy coat of iron gray, fawn, or beige, a long beard hanging from either side of his muzzle, feet that seem riveted to the ground, an oddly turned-up nose, all give the Bearded Collie the amusing look of a large toy. In earlier times, however, he had a far different reputation. Already known in Europe at the time of the Roman invasions, he was, for centuries, a vigilant guard of the flocks, showing a remarkable resistance to the rigors of winter, thanks to his abundant furry coat.

The rare specimens one sees from time to time in shows are still noted for their inherited resistance to cold wet weather. Their ideal height is 21 to 22 inches (53 to 56 cm.).

Bearded Collie

29 The Collie is one of the most beautiful dogs. Faultless of line, with an elegant bearing, expressive even in repose, he is gentlemanly in his relations with others.

Yet until 1860, the Collie led a hard life in the Scottish countryside, looking after the flocks, guarding farms, and generally keeping an eye on things out in the open. All this was before he was noticed by the Queen. It is well known that the British Royal House has always had an enormous influence on the fate of English dogs. Such was also the case with the Collie. In 1860, during a visit to Scotland, Queen Victoria discovered this rough guardian of the flocks and immediately wanted one of her own. From that time on, countless litters of Collie pups were whelped, and twenty years later, the Scottish Sheepdog was popular as far away as the United States.

Like all animals put in the hands of breeders to be developed, the Collie was changed and improved by successive crossings. Although he was already a handsome sheepdog with a long and noble head, the breeders sought to obtain a more beautiful coat, a larger woollier collar, fringes on the legs, the most tapered nose possible, and an even more accentuated nobility. The majority of these improvements worked out well. However, the excessive elongation of the head, which was justified aesthetically, unfortunately impaired the dog's intelligence. Subsequent breeders have remedied this situation. The Collie has regained his intelligence, and today it is common to see individuals whose beauty and intelligence have made them worthy of the description ''the dog with the brains of a man and the charm of a woman.''

The Collie has a long body with an elongated muzzle, almond-shaped eyes, small ears set back on his head, and a long bushy tail. His coat is dense over a thick undercoat and may be tan, tricolor (black, tan, and white), or merle. Height for dogs: 24 to 26 inches (61 to 66 cm.); weight: 60 to 75 pounds (27,3 to 34 kg.). For bitches, height: 22 to 24 inches (56 to 61 cm.); weight: 50 to 60 pounds (22,5 to 27,3 kg.). He is an easily trained dog, affectionate, excellent as a watchdog and bodyguard, and a very pleasant companion.

There is a shorthaired variety of Collie, differing only in his smooth dense coat. At one time, it was believed that they were two different breeds, but the two varieties—longhaired and shorthaired—can appear in the same litter. The shorthaired Collie has been trained as a guide for blind children, and in this role, he has proved incomparable.

Collie (Scottish Sheepdog)

Shorthaired Collie

In eighteenth century England, the Old English Sheepdog was used to drive the livestock to market. Since dogs other than work dogs were taxed, it became the practice to dock the tails of the Sheepdog, so that the tax collectors would not confuse him with a luxury dog. It is thus that the Old English Sheepdog acquired the nickname Bobtail. After generations of docked tails, dogs which were naturally tailless began to appear in litters, and this became an essential characteristic of the breed.

The Old English Bobtail Dog, as it is called in England, is a dog which exudes charm from every hair, and he certainly has plenty of hair falling right down over his eyes. To avoid eczema, this dog needs to be brushed frequently. As his friendly, good-natured eyes can only just be seen under his bushy eyebrows, the Bobtail's vision is limited. But, by way of compensation, his hearing and sense of smell are extremely acute. Characterized by a singular, low-pitched bark, he also has a distinctive and amusing gait. He walks, trots, and gallops with an incredibly light but bearlike motion.

Easy to train, he is equally popular as a pulling dog and a guard dog, and he even served in the army during the Second World War. Today, he is popular as a luxury pet, who loves, above all, to lie at the feet of his master. His sweetness and total lack of nervousness make him the ideal companion for small children.

The Bobtail measures 22 inches (56 cm.) and upward. All shades of gray and blue are admissible, with or without white patches.

Old English Sheepdog (Bobtail)

31 Americans describe this dog as "a beautiful Collie seen through a magnifying glass." He is, in fact, a Collie in miniature, created by crossing a true Collie with miniature breeds local to the Shetland Islands, in the north of Scotland. Old engravings show the Shetland Sheepdog guarding flocks of sheep on rocky hillsides.

Always fulfilling the tasks to which he is set, be it as shepherd or guardian of the farm, the Shetland Sheepdog shows an exceptional aptitude for jumping over fences. He is docile, tireless, and, above all, intelligent. He is a heavy, compact dog with a thick, rough coat of white, red, and black (white must not be the dominant color). His height is 13 to 16 inches (33 to 40,5 cm.).

Today, he is a companion dog, but in the city, he has lost some of the character of his shepherd ancestors and may be nervous.

Shetland Sheepdog

Although of very ancient lineage, the Corgi did not receive official appreciation and recognition until 1934. Once again, credit for this recognition belongs to the English Royal Family. Queen Elizabeth, who was then only a child, was given a pair of Corgis by her father, King George VI. Since then, the droll and likeable Corgi has always lived at Buckingham Palace.

Welsh farmers have used the Corgi to keep the herds in order for centuries. Although small and almost dwarflike, he is hardy, brave, energetic, and able to command respect. He has a singular method for driving cows forward. He leaps at them, giving their rears a vigorous push, and then immediately ducks down to the ground to avoid the inevitable kick delivered by the cow in return.

Today, the Corgi can be found all over Europe and has become an excellent town dweller, adapting to any kind of life or home. Since he possesses, among other qualities, an above-average intelligence, he is very easy to train.

He is approximately 12 inches (30,5 cm.) tall. He has short, strong legs and hair that is thick without being rough. The color of his coat varies from red to sand or may be black and red. White markings are allowed on the chest and legs. The tail is naturally short. The head is like that of a fox, and the more this resemblance is accentuated, the more the dog is prized.

There are two varieties of Welsh Corgi: the Cardigan and the Pembroke, the latter being more popular. In order to help him remain vigorous, happy, and lively to an advanced age, British experts advise that older dogs not be allowed to jump high, as they might injure their long spines.

Welsh Corgi

Cardigan Corgi

33 Of all the Portuguese breeds of sheepdog — Podengo, Castro Laboreiro, Perdigueiro, Cao de Agua — the Rafeiro do Alentejo, from the region of Alentejo, where he gets his name, is the most robust and powerful. His height can exceed 28 inches (71 cm.) and his weight 110 pounds (50 kg.).

Beneath his heavy and phlegmatic appearance, he is a truly remarkable work dog. He has short, thick hair, wise eyes, and a fine, bearlike head. He is aggressive toward strangers and shows a ceaseless vigilance when guarding herds and property. He is an animal that requires little care and can even, if necessary, go several days without food.

Although dogs of this breed are not common, one can find relatively purebred specimens in the Portuguese countryside and in some dog shows. The Rafeiro do Alentejo may be black, tan, yellow, and all these shades in combination with white. Tiger-marked specimens are also common.

Rafeiro do Alentejo

Herd Dogs

While the sheepdog is generally used to protect sheep, the Bouvier, or cowherd, has the more arduous task of controlling herds of cattle. He must, therefore, be stronger, more energetic, and braver, though this does not deprecate the qualities of the sheepdog, who may have the terrifying task of confronting wolf.

The Bouvier des Flandres is the oldest of the Bouviers and is of Franco-Belgian nationality. Resembling the Schnauzer, from whom he is probably descended, he is able to perform the most arduous work and withstand the coldest weather. Intelligent and easily trained, the Bouvier des Flandres was used by the Franco-Belgian troops during the First World War to carry messages and search out the wounded in unprotected areas.

Although he is an unusually large dog, (height, $23\frac{1}{2}$ to $27\frac{1}{2}$ inches (60 to 70 cm.)) he never appears heavy or hulking. His coat is shaggy and wiry, his tail is docked short, and his small ears are clipped triangularly, in such a fashion that they give an enemy nothing to grab onto and cannot get caught in the underbrush.

The Bouvier des Flandres has proved himself especially useful as a watchdog on farms, as a police dog, and as a bodyguard. His coat is generally tawny, black, gray, or grizzled.

A dog with almost the same characteristics is the Bouvier des Ardennes.

Bouvier des Flandres

37 The Appenzell is a Swiss mountain dog like the Entlebuch, the Bernese, and the Great Swiss Mountain Dog. All are also known as draft animals, as they may often be seen pulling small carts of cheese or milk.

The Appenzell is a dog of venerable origin. Descended from the Molossus, he was introduced into the north of Europe by the Romans. In time, he crossbred with the wolf, losing in stature (maximum height, $23\frac{1}{2}$ inches (60 cm.), weight, around 55 pounds (25 kg.)), but gaining in vitality. The breed is ideally adapted to its job of herding cattle in the mountains, driving the cows from one valley to another tirelessly, day and night. While it is true that the Appenzell becomes deeply attached to his master, it is not advisable to try to raise him in town. He is a dog who, by nature, needs to run free in the fields and the mountains.

Appenzell Mountain Dog

38   Although popular in the valleys of Switzerland, the Bernese Mountain Dog has been, for some time, eclipsed by the St. Bernard. Today, however, he is coming back into favor in his old role of companion to the herds and as a loyal and honest watchdog. The ancient Romans also used the Bernese as a fighting dog, equipped with a hard, leather collar encrusted with large iron studs. A little hot blood still remains from this period, and the peace of the herd need only be disturbed for it to be unleashed. Even with the cows he watches, he is not particularly gentle.

    In Germany, the Bernese Mountain Dog has been used successfully as a police dog and rescue dog. His powerfully built body shows that this is a born working dog. His heavy coat, which keeps him warm in winter, does not need any particular care. He is between 23 and 27½ inches tall (60 to 70 cm.) with bitches measuring between 21 and 26 inches (53 to 66 cm.). His name comes from the fact that dogs of this breed used to accompany milkmen to market in the canton of Berne.

Bernese Mountain Dog

39 Of all the herd dogs in Switzerland, the Great Swiss Mountain Dog is undoubtedly the best known. He is much appreciated for his incomparable abilities. As a driver of cows, he dominates his charges completely, always keeping the herd in order and in the right territory. In addition, he is an exceptional guard of the cowshed and a prized protector of his master's house and property. He seldom rests, sleeping at night with one eye open.

He looks very similar to his cousins the Appenzell, the Bernese, and the Entlebuch: same black, reddish brown, and white coat, same general shape, with only small differences in height and consistency of coat. The Great Swiss Mountain Dog is some 28 inches tall (71 cm.). He will willingly haul a light cart filled with milk, children, or golf clubs.

Great Swiss Mountain Dog

Watchdogs

42 Giant of the canine world, the Great Dane was developed in Germany by crossing the English Mastiff and the Greyhound. His English name ''Great Dane'' is a translation of ''Grand Danois,'' one of several names by which the breed was known in France. Why this particular name was chosen for translation is not known. He is also, and more accurately, known as the ''Dogue Allemand,'' or German Mastiff. Whatever he is called, one finds evidence of his ancestors in ancient Greece. A dog looking very like the Great Dane is represented on a Greek coin of the year 36 B.C., earning him the nickname ''Apollo of Dogs.'' Slender, but powerful and remarkably fast, the Great Dane is a majestic, well-proportioned dog. His minimum height is 30 inches (76 cm.), however, a height of 32 inches (81,3 cm.) or more is preferred. The amounts of food, especially meat, needed to feed this dog can make his upkeep a real problem. Paintings of the sixteenth century, a time when he was considered simply a Greyhound, show him hunting wild boar and deer, activities at which he excelled because of his strength, his speed, and his fast reflexes. The Great Dane had its period of greatest popularity in the nineteenth century in England when a horse and carriage was not considered complete unless it was preceded by at least two harlequin Mastiffs. One of the best known German Mastiffs was the one belonging to Bismarck. It accompanied him everywhere, and its death was world news. The modern Great Dane has retained his hunting instincts, but his natural ferocity has been tempered somewhat by breeders. Thus, he adapts very well to city life and even to households where there are children, since he is docile and well aware of his own strength. This handsome and powerful dog is, however, too big for the modern apartment, which is getting smaller and smaller. Today, the Great Dane is highly regarded as a guard dog (he has honorably protected the gold mines of South Africa for years) and as a bodyguard, if only because his huge size commands respect. The Great Dane has short, thick hair all over his body. The color of his coat may be fawn, steel blue, black, or brindle. The harlequin variety has a white coat with small black patches. Except in England, the ears are always carried erect and so are cut during the puppy's first months. English breeders do not crop the ears of their Danes. The tail, which is not docked, is held horizontally like a fencer's foil when the dog is happy.

Great Dane

Tawny
Great Dane

Brindle
Great Dane

Harlequin Great Dane

Great Dane raised in England
with undocked ears

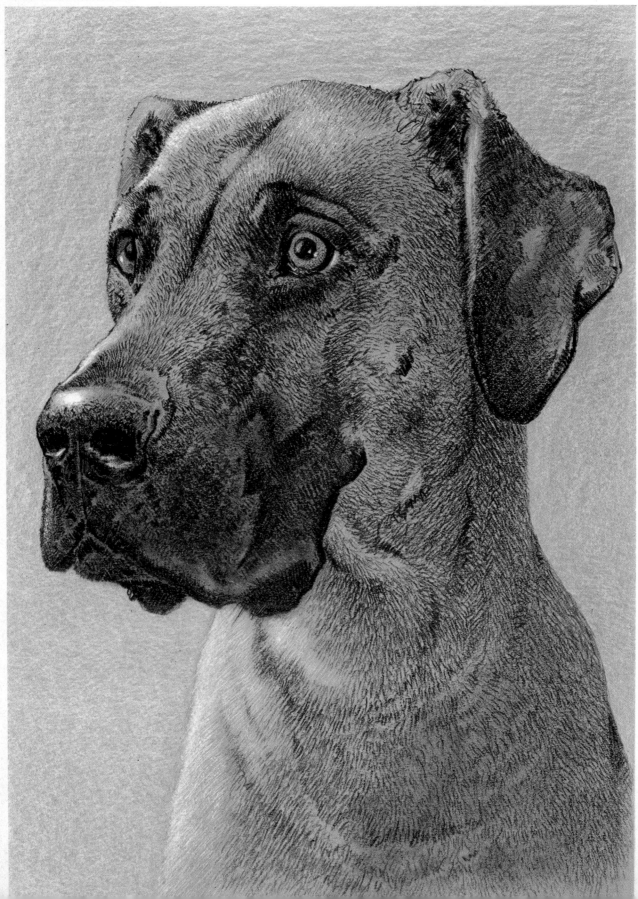

45 The Neapolitan Mastiff can be considered to be the oldest European breed. Nonetheless, his Standard was not fixed until 1943, and he was not shown until 1946, in Naples. The Neapolitan Mastiff is a direct descendant of the Roman Molossus which, in its turn, descended from the celebrated Macedonian Molossus favored by Alexander the Great. The Romans used their Mastiffs mainly for arena fighting where they exhibited a remarkable natural savagery. The breed was "gentled" during the fifteenth century when it was crossed with pointers brought to Naples by the Spanish. From this breeding arose the dog known today as the Neapolitan Mastiff. In the Vesuvian region in particular, the Mastiff found a climate and masters that suited him. He was used by slaughterers to protect their stockyards at night and became the friend and collaborator of criminals. Later, he was used in the army, in the police force, as a draft animal, and as a country watchdog. He remains a formidable adversary, although centuries of breeding have changed his character, making him a good-natured and no longer bloodthirsty dog.

A good-looking dog with a serious and imposing expression, he has quite a striking head with an unmistakable dewlap formed by great folds of skin gathering at the neck. He has round, dark eyes whose brightness depends on the color of his coat, which may be black, blue, tawny, or brindle. His ears are always cropped short so as not to offer a grip to any adversary. His tail too is docked to one-third its length, allowing him to use it to protect his genitals in combat. A courageous dog, the Mastiff will endure physical pain without complaint.

The height of this large, solid dog ranges from $25\frac{1}{2}$ inches to $29\frac{1}{2}$ inches (65 to 75 cm.), $23\frac{1}{2}$ to $25\frac{1}{2}$ inches for bitches (60 to 65 cm.). Some Neapolitan Mastiffs reach and even exceed a weight of 154 pounds (70 kg.). His gait is like that of the bear giving a totally false appearance of slowness.

Neapolitan Mastiff

Although the geneology of this venerable breed is not clearly established, it is certain that the Dogue de Bordeaux, or Bordeaux Mastiff, comes originally from the town of Bordeaux. For centuries, he was used for hunting wild animals: boar, wolf, and bear; and for bullbaiting. Then, as his wilder traits were eliminated by successive breeding, the Dogue de Bordeaux became civilized.

Today, he is a dog of apparently good disposition, faithful, and devoted. He is also an outstanding watchdog. The police have attempted to use him, and he has shown himself to be a gifted police dog, but there is one serious drawback. Once he has caught the criminal, it is useless to order him to let go of his prize.

While not particularly large for a mastiff (height, 23½ inches (60 cm.), weight, 100 pounds (45 kg.)), the Dogue de Bordeaux is a powerful animal with a bulky head. Folds and wrinkles of skin across his muzzle give him a distinctive expression. Coat: tawny, golden, mahogany. Hair: short, fine, shiny.

Dogue de Bordeaux

47 Probably introduced into Italy by the Phoenicians, the Mastiff was welcomed enthusiastically by Caesar's legionnaires and soon became a fighter in the arenas. One can only guess at the remoteness of his origins, since Mastiffs can already be found depicted on Assyrian and Babylonian bas-reliefs. The outstanding qualities of these dogs, however, were first recognized (as is so often the case) by the English, who stabilized and improved the breed. In England, too, the Mastiff was used as a fighting dog and had to defend himself against bulls, bears, and lions. With the abolition of dog fighting in 1835, the breed began to be used for more peaceful ends and developed more and more into a watchdog, a capacity in which he is still used today. Chained up all day and freed at night to roam the farmyards and docks, the Mastiff frightens thieves and other malefactors with his crushing attack and fierce appearance.

The Mastiff has a large head with downturned mouth and pendent muzzle, small ears, and an undocked tail which is borne low. He has a short, dense, rough coat which is fawn, apricot, or brindle in color. Dogs must be a minimum of 30 inches tall (76 cm.); bitches, a minimum of $27\frac{1}{2}$ inches (70 cm.).

Mastiff

The Bull Mastiff breed dates back less than one hundred years, to the end of the nineteenth century, when various experiments with crossing the Mastiff with the Bulldog finally produced a new breed which inherited the best characteristics of each. While the Mastiff is a strong and courageous dog, he is somewhat slow. The Bulldog, also a powerful dog, is lighter and more agile. Their issue, the Bull Mastiff, was, therefore, a formidable dog. Thickset and alert, he made a valuable watchdog. The first to test the remarkable talents of the Bull Mastiff were the English gamekeepers of the late nineteenth century, whose job it was to fight off armed poachers, especially at night. Because of his success, the Bull Mastiff passed into the service of the police. In an England of fogs, gaslights, and ruffians, he performed magnificently, finally becoming the scourge of the London underworld.

Appearing for the first time at a dog show in 1901, the Bull Mastiff was officially recognized as a breed in 1925. In the meantime, however, he had made careers for himself, from gamekeeping to police work and from the army to the diamond companies of South Africa. Very easy to train, and altogether a good big dog, the Bull Mastiff was tentatively accepted into the ranks of family pet, where he proved to be sweet tempered, obedient, and affectionate, albeit mischievous. Nevertheless, he should have a good, firm upbringing and rigorous training, so that his latent aggressiveness never gets the upper hand.

His height ranges from 25 to 27 inches (63,5 to 69 cm.). As in all breeds, the female is smaller and lighter. The coat is short and dense, and its color may be any shade of fawn, brindled or plain. The head is strong and square with a slightly undershot jaw.

Bull Mastiff

Originally from Germany (more precisely from Württemberg, in Bavaria), the Schnauzer's birth cannot be dated exactly. One recognizes him in a painting by Dürer from 1490; one finds him in the court of the Sun King, and again in Stuttgart, in a statue dating back to 1620. In the eighteenth century, it was Schnauzers that accompanied stagecoaches on their long routes through the woods, ready to attack any aggressors, a friend of man and even more of the horse.

The origin of the Schnauzer's name is unclear. *Schnauze* means snout or muzzle in German and was the name of the dog of this breed who distinguished himself in the German Dog Show of 1879.

This is a strong, dynamic dog, very defensive of his master, affectionate, brave, and extremely resistant to illness. Over the centuries, he has been used as a watchdog on farms and in stables, and as a hunter of rats, stone-marten, polecat, and weasel. In German dog shows, any Schnauzer aspiring to a championship must take part in rigorous work trials in which he must flush out fox, rats, and other pests. Because of his innate talents as a hunter, the Schnauzer has always been considered by dog lovers as a member of the terrier family.

The Schnauzer may be black or salt and pepper. His hair is rough and wiry. At least twice a year he needs a special trim, which sets off his charming moustache and bushy eyebrows.

There are three varieties of Schnauzer: the Miniature, the Standard, and the Giant, all of which are bred and registered as separate breeds. The Miniature Schnauzer may be considered a companion dog, while the Standard (the most popular variety) and the Giant are, above all, watchdogs and bodyguards. The height of the Standard Schnauzer should be between 18½ and 19½ inches (47 to 50 cm.). His tail is docked in the first weeks of his life.

Standard Schnauzer

50 This is a little known but interesting German watchdog of uncertain origins. All that is known of his background is that, during the nineteenth century, some landowners devoted to this breed used documents, drawings, and accounts, now lost, to redevelop it. The Hovawart was officially recognized in 1936.

In the Middle Ages, the Hovawart was used for guarding courtyards because of his resistance to inclement weather, his strong jaws, his loud, deep bark, and his rapid and supple gait. He is an excellent runner and jumper of hedges and a good swimmer. He has an outstanding sense of smell, and nothing intimidates him, even when he is trained at an advanced age. A fleeing criminal has little chance against a Hovawart.

His hair is long and slightly wavy. Its color is black, black and tan, or dark blond, sometimes with white patches.

Hovawart

Guard Dogs

The first Boxer was created in Munich, in 1850, by crossing a Bullembeisser Mastiff with a Bulldog. One of his ancestors, however, is pictured in a Flemish tapestry of the seventeenth century. The Bullembeisser, a very ancient breed, was used in bullbaiting and boar hunting, and was, therefore, a strong and ferocious dog. The breeders of the first Boxers thus had to do their utmost to tone down the aggressiveness of the Bullembeisser and to give the new dog a controlled character and make him a reliable companion.

Fundamentally good and loyal, with a sweet and devoted nature, the Boxer is a dog without malice. He is patient with children and well adapted to apartment life, as long as he is frequently given the opportunity to run around outside. He may be trained as a watchdog or bodyguard with excellent results. He has been used by the police and the army and as a guide dog for the blind and has proved the equal of the German Shepherd.

The height of the Boxer may vary from $22\frac{1}{2}$ to 25 inches (57 to 63,5 cm.). His coat is short and shiny. He is a strong-boned dog and can move quickly. His sense of smell is especially keen. Principal colors are yellow, fawn, reddish blond, and brindle. He always has a black mask. The tail and ears are cropped during the dog's first months.

When choosing a Boxer, it is wise to avoid dogs with too fierce an expression, uneven dentation, excessive drooling, too pointed a muzzle, or an unsteady gait. Overly timid dogs should also be avoided.

Boxer

Brindle Boxer

Munich 1850 -
Crossing a Bullembeisser
Mastiff c̄ a Bulldog

Tawny Boxer

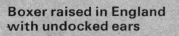
**Boxer raised in England
with undocked ears**

During the second half of the nineteenth century in Germany, a certain Herr Louis Dobermann, tax collector by profession and part-time dog breeder, made frequent journeys through Thuringia with large amounts of money on him. Thus, he conceived the idea of producing a strong, powerful, and agile guard dog which would be able, if necessary, to defend him from thieves. For years, Louis Dobermann worked at this, crossing the very robust French Berger de Beauce with terriers, then with Greyhounds and, finally, with the Weimaraner, and around 1870, he succeeded in producing an intelligent and beautifully shaped animal, but one which was very aggressive. One of the first owners of a Doberman declared: "One must either be brave or stupid to keep one of these dogs in the house."

Officially exhibited in a dog show on 1876, the dog was immediately given the name of his breeder: Doberman. Subsequently perfected by another great German dog fancier, Otto Göller, the Doberman became more elegant, less aggressive, faithful and very good at withstanding damp climates. He quickly became popular in Germany and appeared in all the dog shows of Europe. Apart from his aesthetic beauty, he was particularly liked for the tenacity with which he defended his friends and their property. Like the German Shepherd, the Doberman was adopted with excellent results by the police, the army, and the blind. In the last war, he was the official dog of the U.S. Marines, who used Dobermans to dislodge snipers from trees and ravines in the Pacific islands.

Doberman Pinscher

55   A top-grade Doberman must have a height of between 26 and 28 inches (66 to 71 cm.), with 27½ inches (70 cm.) being ideal, bitches being somewhat smaller. His coat should be short, hard, and thick, and its color may be black, brown, or blue black with a few rust red markings. His ears should be cropped and his tail docked between the ages of three and five months. In dog shows, his gait, which should appear free and nimble, is particularly taken into account. It is also important that he have exactly forty-two teeth. Dobermans require good training, especially when they live with weak or nervous owners. It is said that there is no such thing as a bad Doberman, only a bad owner.

56 The geneology of the Rottweiler is a subject of debate. Some dog fanciers say that he is a descendant of the Bavarian Bouvier, while others claim he was brought to Germany by Caesar's legions and is a direct descendant of the Italian Mastiff. One thing is certain: the breed was in existence during the Middle Ages, because it was pictured in engravings of that time.

The Rottweiler is an exceptionally intelligent dog with an instinct for guard work and, especially, for herding. He is calm and docile and affectionate toward his master and responds well to all types of training. He can be used effectively both for tracking and as an attack dog, and he is valued by the police for his ability to attack on command as well as for his keen sense of smell, thanks to which he can follow a trail for miles even many hours after the quarry has passed.

The Rottweiler has a heavy, well-knit body, as powerful as a bull's. The height of the male varies from $23\frac{3}{4}$ to 27 inches (60,3 to 68,5 cm.), that of the bitch from $21\frac{3}{4}$ to $25\frac{3}{4}$ inches (55,3 to 65,4 cm.). This difference in height between the sexes is often more pronounced in the Rottweiler than in other breeds. His coat is short, black and red with yellow markings. His ears are pendent and unlike his tail, which is docked, they are never clipped. Some Rottweiler pups are born anurous, or without tails.

The Rottweiler is a devoted family dog, but it is essential that he have space in which to exercise.

Rottweiler

57 The Airedale is the largest of the terriers. He is English in origin, and his name comes from Aire, a river in Yorkshire where the first specimens were created less than a century ago by crossing a venerable breed of working terrier with the Otter Hound. Looking like an enormous Wire Fox Terrier, the Airedale is considered a guard dog, even though he inherited from the terrier an excellent talent for hunting. With his long limbs, (he should measure approximately 23 inches (58,5 cm.)), he is not suitable for following his quarry to ground, but in compensation, he is an excellent water dog (this is where his Otter Hound blood comes in).

If he is allowed to run free too long, indications of his ancestral ferocity may begin to reappear. Nothing will stop him then, and he will not hesitate to confront a bear or wolf if necessary. In the home, however, he remains a big puppy all his life. He is patient with children, likes being petted, and will play with anything. He is a true gentleman of a dog. He is not quarrelsome, and only when he is provoked will he display the temperament and teeth of the terrier.

The Airedale was used very successfully as a guard dog during the First World War, when he distinguished himself by his intelligence and courage in carrying out orders.

His coat is short and wiry and is very good protection against bad weather, making him one of the most resistant of all outdoor dogs to winter illness. He should be exercised outdoors a lot and washed frequently. His coat is copper color with large dark patches. He has a muscular neck. His tail is docked to half its length and is held high. His ears are pendent.

Built along the same lines, but smaller, is the Welsh Terrier, a close relative of the Airedale.

Airedale

The Riesenschnauzer is the largest of the schnauzers, probably the result of crossing the Standard Schnauzer with the Bouvier des Flandres and the Great Dane. This contribution of Molossus blood did nothing to lessen his looks, and except for his large size, he looks exactly like the other two varieties of Schnauzer: the Standard and the Miniature.

Bred to perfection by Swiss breeders, who improved his looks, his character, and his height, the Giant Schnauzer can reach and even exceed the height of $27\frac{1}{2}$ inches (70 cm.). His large size makes him somewhat unsuitable as a house dog, and the Standard Schnauzer remains the most popular variety.

The Giant Schnauzer has an impetuous and hot-blooded nature that can be controlled by good training, and as a guard dog, he has no equal. He has also had a brilliant career as a police dog and as an auxiliary to the armed forces. Indeed, during the Second World War, so many Giant Schnauzers died at the side of German soldiers that the breed almost became extinct.

Now, once more very much in vogue, the breed of Giant Schnauzer has been redeveloped in all its majesty. He is able to stand hard work and inclement weather, is above average in intelligence, brave in combat, and boundlessly loyal to his master.

The tail is docked at the third vertebrae, the ears are cropped and held upright, the neck is extremely muscular. The coat is hard and wiry and forms a beard, moustache, and eyebrows. These are complemented by a special trim which is perhaps too frivolous for such a giant dog. The coat is generally black, but salt and pepper dogs are not unusual.

Giant Schnauzer (Riesenschnauzer)

Rescue Dogs

60 The St. Bernard is one of the best-known dogs in the world for intelligence, faithfulness, and usefulness. The finest St. Bernards are found in Switzerland, Germany, England, and America. The breed is a very old one and is probably descended from the Mastiff, which the Roman colonists brought north with them into the Alps two thousand years ago. His likeness can be found on Swiss coats-of-arms of 1350, and it is known that in 1659, the monks of the Hospice of St. Bernard used these dogs to carry butter and milk in the mountains.

Over the years, the monks studied the exceptional qualities of their dogs. They noticed that they had large, flat feet which prevented them from sinking in the snow and that their strength and intelligence were eminently suited to mountain life. Having developed the breed by crossing it with the Pyrenees, the Great Dane, and the Newfoundland, the monks trained the dogs in rescue work. They were taught to search out travelers buried in the snow, dig them out, and warm their faces with their hot breath. If this failed to revive the frozen wayfarers, the dogs were taught to run back to the monastery and raise the alarm by barking. Today, advised by telephone of Alpinists and gypsies, the monks themselves, accompanied by their dogs, go to the travelers' aid. Everyone knows about the cask of brandy distilled by the monks and carried around the neck of the St. Bernard. It was immortalized in a painting attributed to the great painter of dogs, Landseer.

It is estimated that more than three thousand people have been pulled from danger on the snowy paths of Mount St. Bernard by this well-trained dog. One of the most famous is Barry, who saved forty people. Some say he was killed by the forty-first, who mistook him for a wild animal, but others claim that this is a legend and that he was put to sleep peacefully in his old age. More recently, a policeman in South Dakota rescued a St. Bernard who had fallen through the ice on a mountain lake. This is one of the few times man has been known to repay his debt to the St. Bernard.

St. Bernard

Longhaired St. Bernard

61   There are two varieties of St. Bernard: the longhaired and the shorthaired. The latter is more sought after. His short coat leaves him a greater freedom of movement. In the longhaired variety, moisture in the coat may freeze into icicles which weigh him down and hamper his agility.

     The St. Bernard is a veritable giant of a dog. His height is never less than $27\frac{1}{2}$ inches (70 cm.).

     His coat is reddish with white patches or white marked with red, but it is never all one color or without white on it. A dog with a very sweet disposition, the St. Bernard can play for long periods of time without showing the least sign of irritability.

Shorthaired St. Bernard

A veritable mastadon of a dog, the Leonberger was created in 1846 in Leonberg in Württemberg by a German breeder named Heinrich Lessing. He is the result of a carefully planned program of crossings between the St. Bernard, the Newfoundland, and probably the Pyrenees. The exact formula remains a secret. After surviving several periods of neglect, the breed is clearly growing in popularity.

Rescue work and, especially, pulling things out of the water is instinctive with the Leonberger. He has been provided by his Newfoundland ancestors with webbed feet which allow him to swim and float easily. He is an alert, well-balanced, affectionate, and thoughtful dog with gentle brown eyes. The minimum height in males is 30 inches (76 cm.), and he can easily reach 31 inches (78,8 cm.) or even more. His coat is longish, rough, and waterproof. Its color varies from reddish brown to dirty yellow with darker shadows. A white patch is permitted. Some dogs have a black mask.

Leonberger

Crossing a St. Bernard Newfoundland & Pyrenees

63 The Great Pyrenees is a very beautiful and majestic dog. With his great height and his white coat, he resembles the St. Bernard, but he is more elegant. He has a thoughtful look and a natural charm seldom met with in other breeds.

Bold guardian of Renaissance castles, the Great Pyrenees is, above all, a mountain dog. He is an excellent jumper and has displayed outstanding bravery in rescuing people lost in the snow. He is also a formidable adversary for wolf and bear. The Great Pyrenees has been used to improve the stock of the St. Bernard and the Newfoundland, and he is considered their aristocratic cousin. Although he needs a great deal of space for exercise, he adapts well to family life, where he is valued for his loyalty, his sweet disposition, and his fondness for children.

The male should measure 27 to 32 inches (68,5 to 81,3 cm.) at the shoulder, while the female should measure 25 to 29 inches (63,5 to 73,6 cm.).

Great Pyrenees

Newfoundland

The Newfoundland, like the Landseer (a variety of the same breed), is renowned for his instinct for rescuing people from drowning, an instinct that has earned him the title of "St. Bernard of the Water." His origins are not clearly known. When John Cabot discovered the Island of Newfoundland in 1497, there were no dogs of this type there. The island became an English possession in 1583 and the dogs were introduced, but it was not until the eighteenth century that the breed of Newfoundland actually took shape. Raised on this great island of fishermen, the Newfoundland learned to fish himself and was as at home in the water as on land. When he arrived in Europe in 1800, trained for generations in swimming and lifesaving, he was immediately a great success. Americans say that going for a swim with a Newfoundland is a most entertaining experience: he is a wonderful swimmer both on and under water and will play and dive tirelessly.

Countless human lives have been saved by the rescue activities of the Newfoundland. In 1919, a gold medal was awarded to a Newfoundland who succeeded in catching hold of a rope thrown from a lifeboat and then dragging its shipwrecked occupants to shore. In the nineteenth century, there was not a fishing boat or other small vessel that did not have on board at least one Newfoundland. He was affectionately referred to as the "Life-preserver with four feet." The Newfoundland is affectionate with the family, would die for his master, and can safely be entrusted to guard the children, whose games and pranks he endures with endless patience. He is, in short, a docile, good, intelligent, and loyal dog. The poet Byron wrote this epitaph for his Newfoundland: "Beauty without vanity, Strength without insolence, Courage without ferocity, And all the virtues of man and none of his vices."

The Newfoundland is about 28 inches (71 cm.) tall, and his weight is about 150 pounds (68 kg.). His hair is black, sometimes with bluish reflections, and grows thick over his entire body, except that it is somewhat thinner on his head. He has brown eyes and small ears which hang flat against his head; his undercoat, especially in winter, is thick, screening him from the damp.

The Landseer variety of the Newfoundland is very similar to the black Newfoundland. His coat, however, is white with black patches. He was developed by Edwin Landseer, the well-known animal painter. Despite a slightly bearish expression, the Landseer has the same elegant lines and fine character of the Newfoundland. He is a fine swimmer, extremely agile, solidly built, and good with children. Almost extinct during the twenties, the breed was redeveloped in Germany by crossing the St. Bernard and the Great Pyrenees.

Newfoundland and Landseer

Landseer

Sled Dogs

69   Probably descended from the Arctic wolf, these Nordic dogs play different roles, depending upon the people among whom they live. They may be used for pulling sleds, for hunting, or for guarding flocks of caribou, but these are minor differences. The Alaskan Malamute takes his name from the people who lived in Western Alaska, the Mahlemuts, a tribe of highly skilled hunters and fishermen who took great care of their dogs. These dogs, in turn, were exceptionally hardy animals with great prowess as sled dogs over the vast expanses of ice.

Over the centuries, the Alaskan Malamute has been, as he is today, the indispensable companion of his Eskimo masters, loyally enduring with them the privations of Arctic life, sharing their chores, and saving them from danger. The novels of Jack London and J. O. Curwood have made these wonderful animals unforgettable characters. Along with other Nordic breeds, the Alaskan Malamute has taken part in all the polar expeditions from Amundsen's to those of the Duke of Abruzzi. Without their help, these would have been impossible undertakings.

The Alaskan Malamute has an extraordinary sense of direction and can find the right path, even when it is covered with snow. During the long polar night, in the midst of the worst blizzard, he will find the only hut in the entire icy waste. Often used for hunting polar bear, wolf, and moose, he can withstand temperatures of 10 to 16° F. (50 to 60° C.) below zero, protected only by his fur, which is woolly and oily. His ideal height is 25 inches (63,5 cm.) and his weight 85 pounds (38,5 kg.).

Like all Nordic dogs, the Alaskan Malamute is extremely loyal and intelligent. He is docile and clean and does not have a disagreeable odor. He adapts easily to indoor life.

Alaskan Malamute

Very brave and hardy, able to endure temperatures of 16 to 21° F. (60 to 70° C.) below zero, the Eskimo Dog is a great walker and an exceptional sled dog. Had they not had these dogs with them, neither Perry, nor Nansen, nor Amundsen could have made their polar expeditions.

Native to Eastern Siberia, the breed spread to Alaska and Greenland, where even today it is used for hunting polar bears.

The Eskimo is a handsome, likeable, and undemanding dog, with gentle, oblong eyes and an excellent disposition. Work is his only pleasure. He enjoys pulling a sled over the endless expanse of the polar ice pack. He is so strong he can pull a load of twice his own weight. His long coat (the fur may reach 6 inches (15 cm.) in length) lies over a thick undercoat impregnated with natural oils to protect him from the damp. He is a dog that does not bark, but howls like his probable ancestor the wolf.

Eskimo Dog

Of ancient origins, this breed has preserved its purity since prehistoric times. The Samoyed has a strong, muscular body, straight, sturdy legs, magnificent white fur which protects him from the cold, and erect ears on a powerful head. These are the dogs who accompanied the nomadic Samoyed tribes of Siberia, the dogs that gave their lives for explorer Robert Scott and who today live in the region of the North Pole.

It was Robert Scott who, returning from a polar expedition in 1889, brought the first Samoyeds to Europe. The unusual beauty of this dog aroused great enthusiasm among the English, who soon began to breed them. Today, the finest Samoyeds still come from England.

A dog of many capabilities, the Samoyed is useful as a herder and a watchdog, as well as for hunting, fishing, and pulling a sled. When hunting walrus in the harsh Arctic climate, the Samoyed disappears entirely in the snow, where he waits hidden for hours to catch his prey. He is built to withstand the icy air, even for entire nights. He has a shaggy, long coat over a thick undercoat and feet covered with thick tufts of hair, all of which form a screen protecting him from the snow.

He is a marvelous dog and a big winner at dog shows, with his magnificent white or cream-colored coat, his Asiatic face, his mouth that always seems to be on the verge of smiling, and his qualities of courage and tirelessness.

He ranges in height from 21 to 23½ inches (53 to 60 cm.).

Samoyed

The first American explorers called all Nordic dogs Huskies, but the name stuck with that breed which forms such an integral part of man's life in Siberia, the Siberian Husky.

Since the nineteenth century, dog-sled races have been very popular in Alaska. In 1909, a Russian merchant brought some Huskies to Alaska, and they soon became great favorites for both racing and dog shows. The popularity of the Husky quickly spread to America and, more especially, to Canada, where the passion for sled racing has always been lively.

The Husky is a docile and affectionate animal, firm muscled, and extremely resistant to polar temperatures. He is an agile and active animal. His height varies from 21 to 23½ inches (53 to 60 cm.), and his weight is between 45 and 60 pounds (20,5 to 27,3 kg.). Thanks to this light weight, he is a fast racer. His coat is usually wolf gray and silver gray, but all shades are permitted. His eyes are blue or brown, and dogs with one blue and one brown eye are not uncommon.

Husky

Hunting Dogs: Terriers

In the early nineteenth century, a bold type of terrier used to accompany English horsemen on hunts in Sussex for fox, beaver, pheasant, and marmots. This was not the Fox Terrier as we know him, but a small and rather ungraceful dog, who was particularly gifted in hunting vermin into their lairs. The word "terrier," in fact, is French for "burrow."

At that time, all dogs which followed vermin into the earth were called Fox Terriers, but they were far from being the elegant specimens of today. Paintings show us packs of hounds with very different characteristics from those stipulated in the Standard, decreed in 1876. The Standard requires perfectly perpendicular limbs, forward-falling, V-shaped ears, the height at the withers equal to the length of the body between the shoulders and nates so that "it might be inscribed in a square," a height not exceeding $15\frac{1}{2}$ inches (39 m.), and a weight of 18 pounds (8 kg.).

Fox Terrier

Smoothhaired Fox Terrier

This true Fox Terrier, with his attractive appearance and brave temperament, has been popular with people not interested in hunting. An American record company adopted him as a trademark, depicting him with his ear to the horn-shaped loudspeaker of a gramophone, and he was immediately taken up in many households as a family pet. Eager and bellicose in temperament and a great barker, the Fox Terrier has shown himself to be an extremely good guard for house and property.

After being very popular for a long time, the Smooth Fox Terrier made way for his brother the Wire Fox Terrier. Although some purists consider them to be two distinct varieties, the only difference lies in their coats. The rough coat of the Wire Fox Terrier and the particular way in which it is clipped give the dog the appearance of a soft toy, and make him appear totally different from the Smooth. On the other hand, like the Smooth Fox Terrier, he is bold and capable of getting himself killed, rather than giving up the fight. He is extremely intelligent, resistant, and elegant and needs a master who knows how to dominate him without blunting his abilities as a fighter. It is not rare for Fox Terriers to live for sixteen to eighteen years, still keeping themselves slim and in good health.

The tail is docked to a third of its length in the first months of life. This is not merely an aesthetic operation. In fox hunts, when the struggle became bloody, it was important that the tail offer a good grip to extricate the dog from the hole. The fighting qualities of the Fox Terrier are taken into account even at today's shows. Not only is he required to pass hunting tests, but scars do not count against him.

As Vigliardi Paravia, the dog expert, says, "This is the dog with the greatest number of imitators." He is not referring to the many wonderful varieties in the large terrier family, but to all of the mongrels with pitiful tails and bow legs who seem to have at least some Fox Terrier blood.

Both the sleek, hard, thick coat of the Smooth Fox Terrier and the coconut-mat coat of the Wire Fox Terrier must be predominantly white with dark patches of black, blond, or gray.

Smoothhaired Fox Terrier

Wirehaired Fox Terrier

Wirehaired Fox Terrier

76 The Bedlington Terrier is a dog that looks as if it might have been deliberately invented as a lady's pet. His unusual clipping makes him look like a sweet, timid little lamb. But this is a misconception. Americans have described him as the dog with "a lion's heart and a lamb's face." A descendant of the Whippet and the Dandie Dinmont, the Bedlington was raised two hundred years ago by English miners from the village of Bedlington who had anything but drawing room intentions for him. Their companion had not only to hunt fox, badgers, and pheasant, but also, and above all, he had to be a keen adversary of the rat. Down in the mines, rats over nine inches long were common. In 1825, a fourteen-year-old Bedlington that was decrepit, toothless, and blind, managed to draw a badger out of its lair. The old dog was carried off in triumph by the miners and declared the "model Bedlington." After work, the miners organized real competitions in rat-catching, with noisy betting and brawling. On holidays, they turned from rat-catching to racing, and because of this, the dog with the lamb's face is still nicknamed "the miners' racehorse."

Still bred today by miners who mean to keep his primitive gifts of aggressiveness intact, the Bedlington is universally considered a family pet. He is, in fact, affectionate, devoted, intelligent, and proud. He is not quarrelsome and reacts violently only if provoked.

The Bedlington was recognized officially in about 1885. His ideal height, according to the Standard, is $16\frac{1}{2}$ inches (42 cm.), and he must not be under 16 nor over $17\frac{1}{2}$ inches (40 to 44,5 cm.). Bitches are slightly shorter. His weight should be in the range of 17 to 23 pounds (7,7 to 10,5 kg.). He is covered with a coat of thick, rough, cottony hair that is slightly and attractively curly. The coat may be gray blue, liver, or sand, or any of these colors with tan markings. The Bedlington is strikingly different from all other terriers and stands out in the mass of city dogs.

Bedlington Terrier

77 Less handsome perhaps than other terriers and, thus, less popular, the Border Terrier is the smallest member of this large family, weighing 13 to 15½ pounds (6 to 7 kg.). His coat is dense and rough in texture, over an equally thick undercoat. He has a large, flat, otterlike head and powerful jaws.

This dog comes from the frontier between England and Scotland—thus his name, Border Terrier. The soil in this hilly region was extremely suitable for the lairs of the bloodthirsty local foxes. For this reason, it was necessary to create a breed of dog that was small in size but strong and hardy and able to combat the enemy in his underground home. All of these qualifications came together in the Border Terrier. He is eager, untiring, brave, and remarkably persevering. It is unusual for him to miss the prey at which he has been set.

The Border Terrier was officially accepted by the Kennel Club in 1920. He has adapted successfully to home life and is a great friend of children. The colors of his coat may be red, yellow, salt and pepper, or tawny brown and blue with red markings. Clipping is not necessary.

Border Terrier

78 The ancient spectacle of bullbaiting was still popular in England at the beginning of the last century. The most ferocious of the dogs used in those combats was the Bulldog. In 1830, a group of breeders attempted to produce another type of fighting dog: tough and fierce like the Bulldog but better looking, a dog which combined the qualities of agility, beauty, and brutality. They mixed the Bulldog, the white English Terrier, and a touch of Spanish Pointer for height; and the most efficient canine fighting machine was ready—the Bull Terrier. He was a brave bull fighter, a fast dog, and a biter. But laws were passed forbidding this barbaric sport, and the Bull Terrier was forced to take up the same careers as millions of his fellow canines: sheepdog, watchdog, bodyguard, working dog, and companion. He was a great success.

In 1830, he had a brindled coat and the teeth of a wild beast. Twenty years later, breeder James Hinks, by introducing Dalmatian into the breed, succeeded in obtaining an all-white variety similar to the dog we know today. The breed was officially recognized in 1887.

Today the Bull Terrier is known as an unusually obedient dog. He has won innumerable obedience competitions in which he not only had to obey his master's commands, but more important, had to sit still and pretend to ignore the dogs or other animals put next to him to tempt him. He is docile, sweet, overflowing with affection for his family, courteous, intelligent, and agile; but God help anyone who touches his master. This is the one offense the Bull Terrier will not tolerate, and it arouses all his old ferocity.

His body is symmetrical, sturdy, and muscular. He has black eyes of an unusual almond shape. Acceptable colors are pure white (markings on the head are permissible) or any other color with white markings. In the case of colored dogs, the white may not predominate, and all things being equal, brindle is preferred.

Bull Terrier

79 Many years ago in Scotland, graves were covered by symbolic piles of stones. These stone markers, called "cairns," gave their name to a likeable and fearless little terrier. He was developed because a small dog was needed to rout out the wild animals who tended to find shelter in the cairns.

Probably the progenitor of the Scottish Terrier, the Cairn Terrier was once also known as the Wirehaired Skye Terrier. He was first presented publicly in 1902, but he did not become fashionable until 1930. At that time, newspaper reports that the British Royal Family had acquired some pups sent the public rushing to the breeders.

The Cairn's particular gifts are exuberance, liveliness, being a good walker, being easy to train, and being reserved, but never fierce with strangers. His ideal weight should be around 13 to 14 pounds (6 to 6,4 kg.), and his height should be 9½ to 10 inches (24 to 25,4 cm.). He has a thick coat that is somewhat rough to the touch and protects him against moisture, bushy eyebrows, an erect tail, and a foxlike expression. He may be red, sandy, gray, or a very dark (almost black) salt and pepper with darker shadows on the ears and muzzle.

Cairn Terrier

The Dandy Dinmont got his name from a character in a novel. In his book *Guy Mannering,* published in 1814, Sir Walter Scott portrayed a vigorous country gentleman, a sort of rough-diamond type who owned dogs for fox hunting. The novel was very successful, and the dogs that had been background characters, took, in real life, the name of their fictional master, the Scottish farmer Dandy Dinmont. These dogs had existed for at least a century before their appearance in Scott's novel, bred mostly by gypsies and developed, it seems, from various crossings between Old Scottish, Skye, and Bedlington Terriers. There was not a farm in Scotland that did not have one for hunting rats, of which the Dandy Dinmont was and still is a formidable exterminator.

Above all, the Dandy Dinmont is an amusing and extremely likeable dog. Through his thick eyebrows, which fall down over his muzzle, he observes everything with the melancholy look of a clown. And as soon as the occasion presents itself, choosing the perfect psychological moment, he starts playing the fool, striking the ludicrous poses of an old-time buffoon.

A droll and unusual dog, his limbs are so short that he gives the impression of having back legs composed solely of feet. He has a long body, pendent ears, a domed forehead crowned by a sort of topknot, and large, round, intelligent eyes. Lively and brave, the Dandy Dinmont is a born hunter. Underneath his toylike appearance lies a speedy and ferocious enemy of beach marten, polecat, and weasel, and above all, he is a formidable rat catcher.

His height ranges between 8 and 11 inches (20 and 28 cm.), and his weight is between 18 and 24 pounds (8 to 11 kg.). He has long, two-inch (5 cm.), mustard-colored hair. This breed of terrier is raised almost exclusively in England.

Dandy Dinmont

The Irish Terrier has a real Irish temperament. He is so able and fearless in hunting otter, badgers, and wild rabbit that he is called "little daredevil" by the Irish themselves.

He not only knows how to fight on land, but also in water, and he is a fine retriever. He has no equal in tracing down otter or in the unceremonious destruction of water rats. An excellent swimmer, the Irish Terrier can stay in the water even for a couple of hours without adverse effects, thanks to his rough, wiry coat. Like most terriers, the Irish Terrier is a good family pet. He is well mannered, gentle and affectionate toward his master, and happy in the company of children.

In appearance, his affinity with the Wire Fox Terrier is very much in evidence, and they are obviously close relatives. The only clear difference between them is the color of the Irish Terrier's coat, which is red, a shade favored by the Irish. The Irish Terrier's origins go back to pre-Christian times, but it was only in the eighteenth century that he began to show up in paintings, an indispensable element in the green Irish landscapes of grasslands and streams.

"It served bravely, both as a messenger and as a sentry, always distinguishing itself by its boldness and its absolute disregard for danger, often exposing itself to artillery fire." This is a note on the behavior of the Irish Terrier during the two world wars. He was the hero of some of Jack London's novels.

His data: height, 18 inches (45,7 cm.); weight, 27 pounds (12,25 kg.); bitches, slightly smaller. Colors: red, and orange. His docked tail is carried erect. He lives happily both in town and in the country, and in warm or cold climates. As he grows older, he acquires a particular style of dignity and courteousness.

Irish Terrier

82 Like the Doberman and the Landseer, this dog bears the name of his originator, in this case the Anglican pastor Reverend John ("Jack") Russell. He is a terrier developed especially for hunting underground animals. He proved his worth in particular during the last century, working himself down into rocky crevices to rout out vermin with incomparable speed and courage.

   With time, his playful nature and pleasant looks led him to be adopted as a pet. He has a long body, a mottled face, and a wiry coat. However, in the world of dog fanciers he was not received with the same enthusiasm as other terriers. After the death of Reverend Russell, the breed went into a period of decline, and since it has not been recognized by the Kennel Club, it has become somewhat bastardized. In England, however, it is still possible to find purebred specimens.

Jack Russell Terrier

83 At one time, the Irish shepherds in the County of Kerry wanted a dog who would be a good guardian for their flocks, but not cumbersome in size. By repeated, carefully planned crossings of the Irish Terrier, the Dandie Dinmont, and the Bedlington, they produced a new dog: a little daredevil, like the Irish Terrier; a likeable clown, like the Dandie Dinmont; and a fast-moving hunter in sheep's clothing, like the Bedlington. With all this terrier blood in him, the Kerry Blue became a true dog-of-all-work.

Still completely a country dog, the Kerry Blue first appeared in public toward the end of the nineteenth century. The Standard for the breed was fixed by the Irish and the English Kennel Clubs immediately after the First World War. The day that Ireland won its independence, the Kerry Blue became the national dog and began to be called the Irish Blue.

The Kerry is an obstinate but likeable dog—impulsive and affectionate, quick to anger if someone steps on his feet, but just as quick to calm down. He is a most attractive dog. His coat may be any shade of blue, from silver blue to steel blue (it is black until the age of eighteen months when it begins to lighten). The hair is long, slightly wavy, soft, and silky to the touch. He has an elongated head, strong jaws, thick neck, pendent ears, and small, very dark eyes. When he walks, his feet do not bend, giving him a very individual gait. It is common practice all over the world to give him a special trim. Only in Ireland are his coat and undercoat kept intact, and only there is he submitted to work tests.

Today, the Kerry Blue is considered a luxury dog. Though not a common dog, he is much appreciated as a family pet, since he is easy to train and adaptable to city life. He will be gentle and affectionate with the entire family, but he reserves his heart for his master.

Kerry Blue Terrier

This dog resembles the Welsh Terrier except that he is about an inch (2,5 cm.) shorter, and his coat, which is thinner, may be black, blue, liver, black and tan, blue and tan, red, red grizzle, grizzle and tan, or wheaten, instead of only black and tan. He is a small terrier who is easily aroused by the fox in his burrow or the otter in the water. Lakelands have been known to watch their prey underground for ten to twelve days without eating.

Aside from his aptitudes as a hunter, the Lakeland has a playful and affectionate nature and an agile and elegant gait. His height should be between 14 and 15 inches (35,5 to 38 cm.). His weight should be about 17 pounds (7,7 kg.).

Lakeland Terrier

85 Descended from the Black-and-Tan Terrier, this terrier of the same color has been given the name of the British town of his birth. Without doubt, he owes the lightness and elegance of his gait to blood of the Miniature Greyhound, while he inherits from the terrier his sharp intelligence, his speed, and his hatred of rats. This last quality has earned him the nickname "Rat Terrier." No modern pesticide has been able to outdo the Manchester in the destruction of rats.

Light in weight (under 22 pounds (10 kg.)), he has a fine, shiny coat, a naturally short tail, a round head, and a well-balanced body that is at the same time slender and sturdy. He is basically black, with tawny patches distributed irregularly on his head, chest, and legs. The two colors are always distinctly separated.

The Manchester Terrier deserves to be more popular as a pet.

Manchester Terrier

86   The Norfolk is one of the smallest of the terriers, being only 10 inches (25,4 cm.) tall. He is not, however, short on impudence, courage, and liveliness. He stands low on his paws and has a wide skull which is not pointed like that of other terriers. His dark eyes are intelligent and friendly, his ears, pendent. He has muscular thighs and bristly hair that lies flat against his body. The Norfolk is a most uncommon dog and is practically unknown outside England.

Originally bred for hunting vermin, he relentlessly penetrates the smallest lairs. Yet the Norfolk is also an affectionate, unaggressive dog with a well-balanced nature. He is neither easily angered nor subject to nervousness. Only recently recognized by dog fanciers, he will surely gain the affection and appreciation he deserves. The colors of his coat are all shades of red, black, and salt and pepper.

Norfolk Terrier

87 This little Terrier is so lively that he cannot hold still even when he sleeps. It is as if he were charged with electricity. He is an ideal companion for sportsmen and young people. The students at Cambridge University have chosen him as a mascot.

He appeared in 1880 under the name of Jones, his breeder. Later he was given the name of his native town of Norwich. Almost extinct during the First World War, the breed was redeveloped by crossing Bedlingtons, Bull Terriers, and Irish Terriers.

His ideal height is 10 inches (25,4 cm.) at the withers, and he has a foxlike face, strong jaws, and stiff straight hair which may be red, reddish black, or salt and pepper. He is keen on underground hunting, very hardy, friendly, and devoted to his master. The bitch, which has a very protective nature, is the first to train the puppies for hunting.

Norwich Terrier

The Scottish Terrier is one of the most amusing and endearing dogs. He appears on whiskey labels and greeting cards and is a favorite of toy makers and children who think of him as a living toy. Intelligent, lively, and high spirited, he is as proud as a Scotsman in a kilt. He is independent and quick to bare his teeth when annoyed. It is better to teach him obedience at an early age than to be forced to use a muzzle, which would only spoil the attractiveness of his bearded face.

Known in eighteenth-century Scotland as a hunter of fox, wild rabbit, otter, and badgers, which he routed out with amazing skill, he has today become domesticated without losing his ancient instincts. Given the chance, he will dig holes in the ground and behave aggressively toward other animals. He is an excellent watchdog, with a strong bark worthy of a much larger dog. He has a solid, strong, hardy body with hard nails and powerful jaws. The English have described him as "a big dog in a small space."

His height should be about 10 inches (25,4 cm.), and he should weigh about 19 to 22 pounds (8,5 to 10 kg.). Three colors are permitted: black, brindled gray, and yellowish brown (most unusual). His coat, which is extremely thick in cold countries, consists of a bristly outercoat over a thick soft undercoat. To maintain the beauty of this coat, the Scottish Terrier requires a special treatment called stripping, which consists of pulling out excess hair tuft by tuft. This may be done two or three times a year without harming the dog.

He gives his love and loyalty to a single master almost exclusively. It is necessary to watch his feeding carefully as he is subject to eczemas. Between 1929 and 1944, the Scottish Terrier was one of the most popular dogs in the world.

Scottish Terrier

"The happy union of gaiety and courage," one could not find a better definition of the Sealyham Terrier, a small, white Fox Terrier developed by Captain John Edwards of Sealyham Castle, Wales. Although he was bred to be a spirited hunter of vermin, the Sealyham has also kept the gay humor he inherited from his ancestor the Dandy Dinmont. A skillful blend of Flanders Basset Hound, Dandy Dinmont, Corgi, and the rough-haired West Highland White Terrier resulted in this adorable little dog with short legs and a special instinct for underground hunting.

Originally the Sealyham's coat was reddish. Thus he was easily confused with the fox and got many of the bullets intended for it. He was also in danger of being bitten or even killed by the Bloodhounds with whom he hunted. Further breeding with the Bull Terrier gave him an all-white coat, and such errors were no longer possible. His hair, therefore, is white or white marked with yellow. It is as hard and wiry as the bristles of the boar, over a soft undercoat. His thick, prominent beard gives him a highly individual look. His average height is $10\frac{1}{2}$ inches (27 cm.), and his weight is around 23 pounds (10,5 kg.). Bitches are slightly smaller. He has lively, almond-shaped eyes, ears which fall forward onto his cheeks, short powerful legs, a docked tail which is held erect, and a compact agile body.

Like almost all the terriers, the Sealyham has become a pet. He is affectionate, funny, aristocratic, intelligent, quick to catch on to what he is taught, and executes commands with his characteristic sense of humor.

Sealyham Terrier

90   It is said that at the beginning of the seventeenth century, a Spanish ship was wrecked on the rocks of Scotland and that among the survivors there were some Maltese dogs. These dogs subsequently mated with local terriers and gave rise to a new breed, the Skye Terrier, named after the island in the Hebrides where they were developed. Although this story is certainly credible, there is another theory which seems to prevail: that of the dog fanciers who see in the Skye Terrier a cross between the Scottish Terrier and the Dandy Dinmont. The Skye Terrier's honorable career as a rat catcher and hunter of foxes is not as long as that of other terriers. His very special beauty destined him to a life in the drawing room. And he did very well for himself in this respect. Queen Elizabeth I acquired some splendid Skyes, and Queen Victoria was also devoted to them.

    The cause of all this admiration is the Skye Terrier's magnificent, thick coat which falls to the ground on both sides, covering him completely, and hiding his already small feet. His head, and even his ears, which may be held upright or pendent, are hidden by thick hair that leaves only a small space free for his tongue to stick out. The color of this unusual coat (which is thick enough to protect him from possible bites) is blue gray, dove gray, or cream, although all shades are allowed, providing that the nose and ears are black.

    Measuring from his nose to the end of his tail, the Skye Terrier is about four times as long as he is high. He measures about 10 inches (25,4 cm.) at the shoulder.

    Despite his origins as a hunter and the strong jaws that he still has, the Skye Terrier is not a biter, and he enjoys the company of children. Like all pets with long hair, he needs frequent brushing and baths.

Skye Terrier

91 This Irish terrier, with soft hair the color of wheat, is a recently recognized breed. He made his debut in the Irish Kennel Club Championship Show in 1937. But he has not yet managed to become well known, either because of the scarcity of breeders or because of competition with other terriers of greater beauty and immediate appeal, or perhaps because of the length of his name.

He is a sturdy but agile dog, full of vitality, as resistant to fatigue as he is to bad weather. He is capable of living indoors or in the yard, which permits him to exercise his innate talents as a watchdog. His coat is thick, with waves like those of the Kerry Blue. Only one color is permitted : the color of ripe wheat. All other shades are considered a serious fault and would disqualify him in a show. He should be 18 to 19 inches (45,7 to 48,3 cm.) tall and weigh 35 to 45 pounds (16 to 20,5 kg.). The Irish consider him their third terrier, after the Irish and the Kerry Blue.

Soft-Coated Wheaten Terrier

This is a very old breed containing Bulldog and terrier blood. Like many other dogs, the Staffordshire Bull Terrier played a part in writing the ugly history of dog fighting, which is still being carried on secretly in English mining towns. Eclipsed for a time by the Bull Terrier, he has enjoyed a resurgence of popularity in England and America where the larger varieties have been bred. His height is between 14 and 16 inches (35,5 to 40,6 cm.) his weight between 28 and 38 pounds (12,7 and 17,2 kg.). He has smooth hair that lies flat against his body. It may be tawny, white, black, blue, or any of these colors with white.

While retaining his fighting nature, he also has the precious ability to distinguish between men and animals and between harmless beings and those with bad intentions. He is a loyal dog who knows how to play with children and who would give his life for his master.

Staffordshire Bull Terrier

93 He looks like a little Airedale, and indeed, he is descended from this breed by way of crossing with other terriers. But he has a very individual personality, and it has been said that of all terriers the Welsh Terrier has the best manners. He is a dog who is well suited to family life because he is happy, lively, affectionate, and obedient. But he has kept the temperament of a hunter of burrowing animals, which he was originally bred to be. Should he find himself in the presence of the proper game, all his warrior instincts are immediately reawakened. Originally, Welsh Terriers hunted together with Bloodhounds, who, with their noses to the ground, would follow the scent of the fox until they found his lair. It was then the Welsh Terrier's job to rout out the underground quarry, and for this he was as much appreciated as the Fox Terrier.

His coat is thick and hard and is either black and tan or brindled black. It needs special clipping when the dog is to be entered in a show. The height at the shoulder should be 15 inches (38 cm.) and his weight is about 20 pounds (9,1 kg.). The Welsh Terrier was officially recognized in 1885 and has since then attracted a growing number of admirers.

Welsh Terrier

The West Highland White Terrier is a relatively young breed that was first exhibited in 1890. His creator, the English Colonel Malcolm, a breeder of Cairn Terriers, seeing that albino pups occasionally appeared in his litters, bred his dogs especially for this characteristic. The Cairn is red or salt and pepper, the West Highland White is totally white; this is the only difference between them.

Small in stature (11 inches tall (28 cm.)), the West Highland is always in motion and on the lookout for a fight. He is especially daring when given the chance to hunt like a terrier. As a pet, the West Highland has shown himself to be more interested than other terriers in sofas and fancy houses where he can enjoy long periods of rest. Being the only small, white Scottish Terrier, he has been pictured along with the black Scottish Terrier on the label of whiskey bottles. He is an independent, stubborn, and unyielding dog and does not make a good watchdog.

West Highland White Terrier

95 The Jagdterrier is a hunter and one of few breeds which has to undergo work tests in order to be judged a champion. In his creation, the result of crossings between various English terriers, a step backward in time has been taken. There is no weakness or ambiguity about this dog's character, no interest in cushions or games, only determination and courage in facing wild animals.

His height is under 16 inches (40,6 cm.). His weight ranges from 20 to 22 pounds (9,1 to 10 kg.) and is about 15 percent less in bitches. But he is not intimidated by the size or impressiveness of his enemies, and would not hesitate, if the situation arose, to combat a rhinoceros or an elephant, even if it cost him his life. In addition, the German Hunt Terrier is obedient and loyal to his master. He may be used to hunt in water or as a retriever, and to point out the spore of wild animals.

German breeders have faith in the future of this aggressive dog, considered bad tempered and even ferocious by some. They will only allow the breeding of dogs with the right credentials : if a Jagdterrier shows the least sign of trust or affection toward a stranger, he will remain celibate for life.

There are two varieties of German Hunt Terriers : one with rough hair, and one with smooth. Both are immune to the illnesses common to wild animals. The coat is predominantly black, or brown with red patches.

German Hunt Terrier (Deutscher Jagdterrier)

96 This is one terrier among many that are called "Australian." The breed originated in Australia as a result of crossing a number of terriers imported from England, probably the Yorkshire, Skye, Norwich, Cairn, and Manchester. From each of these ancestors the Australian Terrier has taken something : his unusual silvery blue color, the roughness of his coat, his short legs, his liveliness. His body is long in relation to his height (10 inches (25,4 cm.)). His docked tail is carried high. His eyes are dark and flashing. In spite of his aptitudes, the Australian Terrier is not used for hunting, but is exclusively a pet. The breed was recognized in 1933.

Australian Terrier

The Silky Terrier is a cousin of the Australian Terrier. Despite the fact that the breed dates back to the beginning of the twentieth century when it originated in Sydney, Standards for this dog have only recently been fixed. As his name indicates, he is covered with a silky coat which may be silver blue or blond beige. He is about an inch (2 to 3 cm.) shorter than the Australian Terrier.

Like the Australian Terrier, the Silky Terrier is a sturdy dog that has become exclusively a pet. He has not, however, renounced the irreverent nature of the terrier. To maintain his beauty, his coat needs constant care.

Silky Terrier

The Basenji, or Congo Dog, as his name indicates is a native of Africa. One finds the earliest traces of the breed on Egyptian tombs and inscriptions five thousand years old. Discovered by European explorers, the first Basenjis were brought to England at the end of the nineteenth century, but they did not survive. A later, more successful attempt was made in 1937. In his native land, the Basenji is prized by his African masters whom he serves as a guide. He has proved himself to be an excellent tracker, an expert at warning of the presence of ferocious beasts, and a hunter of small game. Because of his agile grace in jumping over the tall grass, he has been compared to a little fawn.

He is 16 to 17 inches (40,6 to 43 cm.) tall, and weighs about 22 to 24 pounds (10 to 11 kg.). He has a short, shiny coat which is fawn, chestnut and white, black, black and white, or reddish tan with white patches. He has erect ears and a curled tail and looks very intelligent, because the wrinkles on his forehead give him a strangely pensive look. He is affectionate toward his master and a great friend to children.

Basenji

Hunting Dogs: Dachshunds

He seems as if he might have come straight from the pencil of a modern cartoonist, but the breed of Dachshund is several thousand years old. The Germans call him Teckel because of his resemblance to the dog "tekal" depicted on the funeral statue of a pharaoh. However, in Latin America, too, there are numerous drawings of a similar little dog with a long body. Experts believe that the Dachshund got his shape from centuries of hunting small animals down into their lairs. In the course of generations, a mutation of extreme shortness appeared—a sort of localized rickets. This characteristic was passed on by heredity and resulted in a new variety of dog that became standardized in Germany. There, the careful process of selective breeding began in the eighteenth century, the subsequent fixing of the characteristic of shortness, and the perfecting of the three types of Dachshund—shorthaired, longhaired, and wirehaired—earned this amusing dog the name German Basset. It is said that he is as long as two dogs and as tall as half a dog. He risks being stepped on since he is only 14 inches tall (35,5 cm.) at most, with the miniature variety reaching only 8 inches (20 cm.). His weight depends on his variety. The larger Dachshund weighs 22 to 24 pounds (10 to 11 kg.), the standard $16\frac{1}{2}$ pounds (7,5 kg.), the miniature 9 pounds (4 kg.).

Endowed with powerful jaws, an extremely fine sense of smell, courage, and tenacity, the Dachshund is an excellent hunter of vermin. If the entrance to the lair is too small he will enlarge it by persistent digging with his nails, and he can wait days and days until the quarry, driven by hunger, emerges from his den in search of food. It is then that the Dachshund will engage it in awesome battle. The strength of his adversary does not frighten him. He is not always victorious, but he would rather die than flee. The popularity of the Dachshund is still great in Germany, England, and Switzerland, where he is raised and used for hunting wolf, badger, hare, and even in packs for wild boar and roebuck, since he is an excellent tracker. But one also finds a growing number of breeders who raise Dachshunds solely as pets, and who, therefore, produce docile, gay, affectionate little animals, whose former temperament only occasionally reappears.

The Dachshund suffers from the cold of winter, especially in northern countries, and he becomes reluctant to leave his warm corner. It is, therefore, a good idea to see to it that he is frequently exercised (perhaps protected by a little jacket) so that he does not become sluggish. In spite of his puppetlike appearance, he is an excellent watchdog.

In the shorthaired variety of Dachshund, the preferred colors are reddish black, reddish brown, and orange with possibly some small black markings. The longhaired Dachshund differs from the shorthaired variety only in his coat, which is long and silky and covers him completely, right down to his fringed paws. The third variety, the wirehaired, is identical to the other two except for his rough coat, bushy eyebrows, and endearing beard. There exists also another, less prized variety of Dachshund, the "harlequin," with a strangely marked brindle coat.

Dachshund

Shorthaired Dachshund

Miniature

Longhaired Dachshund

Miniature

Wirehaired Dachshund

Miniature

Hunting Dogs: Hounds

104 The bloodhound is a hunting dog that pursues game by natural instinct. As well as an exceptionally keen nose, he has good vision and hearing and is virtually tireless. Bloodhounds generally hunt in packs. The finest of all bloodhounds were those bred in the nineteenth century by the hunters of the German town of Hanover in Saxony. Known since the Middle Ages, the bloodhound was perfected over the centuries by breeding with the Harz Dog, which is no longer raised.

A very tall dog (over 26 inches (66 cm.)), his weight varies from 88 to 106 pounds (40 to 48 kg.). He has an elongated body, a wrinkled forehead, a large and prominent nose, drooping jaws, and soft but energetic eyes. The color of the Hanoverian Schweisshund, as dictated by the German Standard, is gray brown, red brown, orange, or dark yellow. White markings are categorically excluded.

Hanoverian Schweisshund

105 He takes his name from St. Hubert, the saint who made him popular in Belgium in the eighth century, a time when princes and bishops alike delighted in the sport of hunting. When the Normans invaded England, they brought the St. Hubert Hound from Belgium to the island that is now his home. He became known as the bloodhound because even a drop of blood from wounded game provides enough scent to enable him to pursue his quarry, no matter how far the animal may go. He has been humorously described as "a dog behind a nose."

His exceptional sense of smell has also been put to even better use. The Bloodhound has found countless buried precious objects which have been hidden underground, and police all over the world have utilized hundreds of his breed. The work of the Bloodhound is so reliable and precise that American courts accept his dumb testimony as circumstantial evidence. From the point of view of the police, however, he has one grave defect: once he has set the police on an important track, he is determined to finish the job his way and to deal with the criminal as he wishes. He is, in other respects, a naturally good, very gentle, wise, and well-mannered dog.

The Bloodhound is a big dog: about 26 inches (66 cm.) tall and weighing about 90 pounds (41 kg.). He has a large head and rough loose skin which forms heavy folds on his forehead and on either side of his muzzle, like drapes. He has very dark, somber eyes with eyelids that reveal the conjunctiva. His coat is short and is either reddish black or red.

Bloodhound (St. Hubert Hound)

106 The Karelian Bear Dog is a sturdy, muscular, and tenacious dog that is endowed with great courage, a lively gait, and a readiness to obey commands. He comes from the region of Karelia in Finland, where for centuries he hunted moose, roebuck, and hare and fought the wolf. His height varies from 21 to 23½ inches (53 to 60 cm.); a little less for bitches.

    Over the last decades, the principal breeders of Karelians, the Russians, have tried to strengthen the breed to give it the power and aggressiveness needed to fight bears. Thus the Karjalankarhukoira (this is its original Finnish name) has become a Russian bear dog, through, it seems, crossing with the Utchak Sheepdog, an intrepid animal who has no fear of fighting wild beasts. This new Russian version of Karelian Bear Dog not only warns the hunter of the presence of bear, but does not hesitate to attack him and put him to flight. He has a conical head, straight hair, a curved tail, and a black coat with white patches.

Karelian Bear Dog

107 It is said that the bloodhound is a breed as old as man, that when one fine day man decided to hunt in order to live, the very next day there was a bloodhound at his side, helping him track down his prey. The aristocratic Grand Bleu de Gascogne was created by crossing the bloodhound and the St. Hubert Hound. In Gascogne, he found an ideal hunting ground: the marshes (as they existed in the nineteenth century), the famous moors of sand and dunes, the fertile valley bottoms, and the austere foothills of the Pyrenees. There he distinguished himself for speed and unmatched courage.

Described by French dog fanciers as "the most noble of all French hunting dogs and of all tracking dogs in the world," the Grand Bleu is an unusual dog. He is a large dog, about 31 inches (78 cm.) tall, with a very noble head. He has a clear, strong voice that can be heard at a great distance, a sweet, sad expression, round, hard feet like those of a wolf, and a superb sense of smell. The blue color of his coat, from which he gets his name, is unique. Basically white, his coat is finely flecked with black, and it is this subtle mixture that gives off slate blue reflections.

It is rare today to find really purebred Grand Bleus de Gascogne. However, some French breeders have succeeded in preserving this noble breed.

Grand Bleu de Gascogne

It was Baron Joseph de Carayon-Latour de Virelade who,in the region of Saintonge, created this noble breed by crossing three of the best French hunting dogs (the Saintongeois, the Bleu de Gascogne, and the Ariégeois). After long and intelligently planned selective breeding, the Gascon-Saintongeois showed that he had,inherited the best qualities of his progenitors. As well as hunting small wild animals, he soon proved that he was capable of superior tasks, confronting roebuck and, above all, the wolf, which has gradually been disappearing in France because of these tenacious hounds.

The Gascon-Saintongeois, which is also called the Virelade, has very short, fine hair, a white coat that is flecked and marked with black, and a long nasal tract that ends in a wonderfully large, black, turned-up nose. The skin is pink under the white hair and black under the black hair. Unfortunately, the breed has undergone deplorable degeneration due to the carelessness of hunters, and it is quite rare today to find really purebred Virelades.

Gascon-Saintongeois (Virelade)

109 This is a breed which has existed for almost three hundred years. It was created by the Marquis François de Larrye in the ancient French province of Poitou whose historical capital is the city of Poitiers. Here, the Poitevin was developed by crossing local bloodhounds with the Foxhound. Very quickly, he showed himself to be an intrepid hunter in the marshes, in the broom covered meadows, and on the high plains assailed by harsh winter winds. But when the French Revolution came, throwing all of Europe into confusion, it did not spare the packs of hunting dogs which were dispersed and almost totally destroyed. They were redeveloped in the nineteenth century, and the Poitevin reappeared, with the same strong voice, sensitive sense of smell, dedication to hunting in the brush, distinction, and shyness as before.

The Poitevin's height varies between $23\frac{1}{2}$ and $27\frac{1}{2}$ inches (60 to 70 cm.). The coat is tricolor with black patches. Like the Grand Bleu de Gascogne and the Gascon Saintongeois, truly purebred Poitevins are not easy to find.

Poitevin

This is a breed of fairly recent creation that continues to arouse a growing interest because of its particular vocation for hunting roebuck. The Billy is a well-balanced dog, distinguished for his exceptional sense of smell. He is able and cunning in routing out wild animals, unmindful of the wounds that he may incur from direct contact with his prey or thorny briar bushes. The Billy seems to have assimilated the best qualities of the three hounds from which it descends: the Céris, which is effective with wolves; the Montembeouf, which is muscular and resolute when facing wild boars; and the Poitevin, which is excellent for any game.

The Billy can make himself heard even from a great distance, modulating his pleasant voice according to the importance of the prey which he has sighted. He has ears that are set high and fall toward his neck. His coat is very short and hard and sensitive to intense cold. Its color can be white, café au lait, white with orange patches, or white with lemon patches. When not working, the Billy is a quarrelsome dog.

Billy

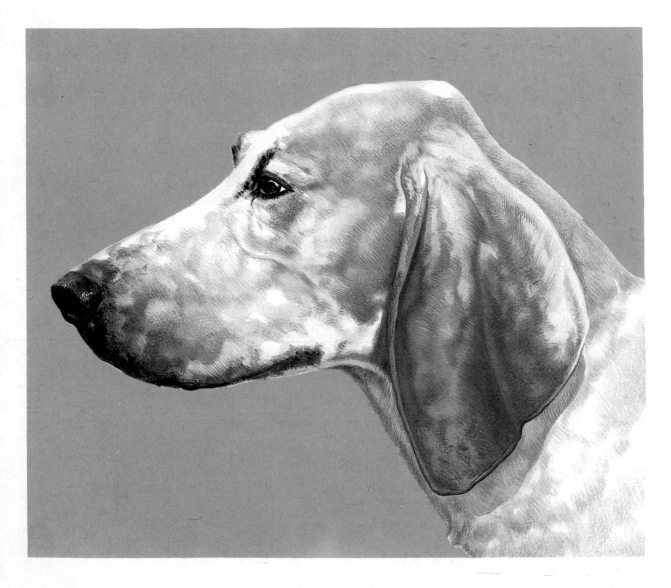

111 This is a very large, well-balanced dog, big boned but distinguished looking, which descends from the ancient Gascon and Saintongeois breeds crossed with the Foxhound. The contribution of his ancestors is always clearly dominant. He is accustomed to working in packs and excels in hunting deer and roebuck. Seeing him let loose with his angry bark, one might well think him a ferocious dog. But, on the contrary, he is a sweet and obedient animal who works like a professional in harmony with man. He is tough when hunting, but gentle at home.

There are three varieties of the Chien Francais: the white and black, which is the most common; the tricolored; and the white and orange, which is rare. He is a good-looking dog, especially in the animation of the pack. He has a lively expression, a long nasal tract like that of a sheep, large ears, and an elegant gallop. He is 24 to 28 inches (61 to 71 cm.) tall. The Standard for the breed was fixed in 1957.

Chien Francais

112 The Elkhound is one of the most ancient breeds, having remained the same for thousands of years. When Stone Age man hunted in the woods of Scandinavia, there was a dog at his side, and skeletons found in a stratum of the earth which goes back to 4,000 or 5,000 B.C. show that he was identical to the Elkhound of today. With the Vikings, the Elkhound hunted bear and elk and then proved to be equally valuable for pursuing marten, ermine, and grouse, for watching over the flocks, for pulling sleds, and guarding homes. But his name is, above all, linked to elk hunting: the dog picks up the elk's scent at a distance of two and a half to three miles (4 to 5 km.), and from there, he watches the movements of his prey. Silently the Elkhound blocks the elk's path and then drives it toward the hunters, who are guided by his special bark. If the elk attacks him with its powerful horns, the Elkhound evades it with the narrow movements of a bullfighter, changing the tone of its voice to convey that things are getting more dangerous and that the moment has come to slaughter the prey. The Elkhound is also very much appreciated as a sled dog. In Norway, he has been trained by the army to transport equipment and provisions in the snow.

Although this docile and intelligent Nordic hunting dog adores leaping around in the fresh air, he can become an excellent domestic pet, as he is loyal, very clean, odorless, affectionate, lacking in neuroses, and easily trained. The Norwegian Elkhound measures about $20\frac{1}{2}$ inches (52 cm.) and weighs around 55 pounds (25 kg.). He has a thick coat of heavy, waterproof hair in all shades of gray.

Elkhound

Norwegian Elkhound

113   The Swedish Elkhound (Jämthund) is very similar to the Norwegian variety but slightly bigger. He measures 23 inches (58,5 cm.) in height, weighs 66 pounds (30 kg.), and has a gray or black coat. He is energetic and very brave when hunting, but also very obedient and gifted, with a great sense of balance. During the warm months, Elkhounds living in the city require careful cleaning of their coats to prevent skin disturbances.

The Foxhound is, as its name implies, a bloodhound used for fox hunting. He is descended from the ancient Norman Bloodhound crossed with the Greyhound to increase his speed, with the Bulldog to give him more strength, and finally, with the Fox Terrier to equip him for a specialized form of hunting.

By skillful selective breeding, breeders perfected the Foxhound, using only the most harmoniously proportioned, the bravest, and the most energetic specimens as studs. Thus, at the beginning of the nineteenth century, the Foxhound represented the acme of hunting-dog breeding and was used especially by the English aristocracy for fox hunting on horseback. There is a vast collection of illustrations in which horsemen in red and blue outfits are depicted rushing through the English countryside preceded by stags and surrounded by happy packs of Foxhounds.

It is said that this is a dog capable of tiring out ten horses. Indeed, he can run around an area of ninety-three square miles (150 sq. km.) without stopping from dawn to dusk, finally returning home, perhaps in the middle of the night, with energy to spare, after lingering over the last lap. In general, obstacles will not stop the Foxhound, whether they be marshes, the most impenetrable bramble bushes, or the most cantankerous animals. He will face any difficulty at the risk of coming out of it grazed or wounded. For some time, he was the only dog whose ears the English allowed to be cropped to prevent them from being torn by thorns or foxes' teeth, but recently, the rule applying to other hounds in Britain has prevailed, and ears are no longer cropped. Thus, he has regained his original appearance, with his wide ears falling against his cheeks. He has a smooth, hard, shiny, tricolored coat (black, white, and red) or bicolored (a white background with patches of ore and other colors).

Foxhound

English Foxhound

115   His height should not be less than 22 inches (56 cm.) and never more than 24¾ inches (63 cm.). His weight should be around 66 pounds (30 kg.).

Foxhound owners say that the dog must be well trained, as he has a tendency to regard the game as his own, and he will carry off his prey to be devoured at leisure. This is a defect that would dishearten any huntsman, but one that can easily be rectified by good training.

The American Foxhound is lighter than his English cousin, but has the same characteristics. He was used for hunting down Indians, In 1770, George Washington himself bought a pack of English Foxhounds and proceeded to cross them with a variety of greyhound (the Staghound) given to him by Lafayette, the French general. It appears that it was from this Washington-Lafayette crossing that the American Foxhound originated. Since the American fox lives in vaster and wilder territories than his European counterpart, breeders have given their Foxhounds a more acute sense of smell and a still greater speed in running. When a dog is let loose in the meadows, there is no horse that can keep up with him, and it is common for the Foxhound to suddenly find himself lost and alone. For this reason, American breeders have given him a stronger voice than that of his European cousins. His full-bodied tenor will carry for miles and is also pleasantly melodious. There are popular songs which have been inspired by the Foxhound's voice.

American Foxhound

116   Germany possesses a whole series of excellent bloodhounds. One of the most tenacious of these is the Dachsbracke. There are two varieties of Dachsbracke, the Westphalian Basset and the High Mountain Basset, which differ only in size: the first being $11\frac{3}{4}$ to $13\frac{3}{4}$ inches (30 to 35 cm.) tall and the second $13\frac{3}{4}$ to 16 inches (35 to 40 cm.) tall. Officially recognized in 1886, the Dachsbracke is a small dog somewhat like the Dachshund, with an endearing face but a strong-minded nature. He is mostly used in difficult, rocky areas for hunting hares and foxes. He is also put on the trail of larger game like deer and roebuck, and the little, long-bodied Dachsbracke will willingly take on even wild boar. A multi-talented hound, however, he does not disdain bringing back small game.

    He has pendent ears, a long-fringed tail, and short flat hair that is thicker on his neck and back. Among the most common colors are black with red markings, brown with light streaks, and yellow red.

Dachsbracke

117   Spaniels are pointers. Their way of hunting is to stop and freeze when they come across game,
pointing it out clearly to the hunter. The German Spaniel, raised at the beginning of the twentieth
century by Friedrich Roberth, is a mixture of small and large dogs whose common characteristics were
having long hair and being able to seek out game in the brush. From these breeds emerged the
German Spaniel, which is intelligent and sweet tempered with man, but vigorous and unyielding with
game. He is an instinctive retriever and fearless both of water and thorny bramble bushes. It is not rare
for a German Spaniel to stop and point at the game and then, before the hunter has a chance to
intervene, to attack and bite its prey in the neck.

The German Spaniel is 18 to 19½ inches (45 to 50 cm.) tall (bitches are slightly smaller) and has a
thick and wavy coat, a long-fringed tail, very acute vision, and an infallible sense of smell. Possible
colors for the coat: brindle, brown, and deer red.

German Spaniel (Wachtelhund)

The hound is a dog that has undergone a lot of regional modifications. In Austria, for example, the Tyrolean, the Styrian, the Bavarian Mountain, the Swiss, the Lucerne, the Bernese, the Bruno, etc., are all types of hounds bred by hunters with the characteristics of their areas in mind.

One of the most appreciated local hunting dogs is the Tyrolean hound, the Tiroler Bracke, which was bred expressly to work in the mountains in all seasons. It is a Dachshund-like, muscular, and fast moving dog that follows tracks tenaciously and may also be used as a pointer and retriever. In addition to all this, he is efficient as a watchdog, and, being about 16 inches (40 cm.) tall, he does not get in the way.

The Tiroler Bracke has strong teeth, large eyes, wide, thin ears set high, and a straight tail that he holds erect during the hunt. His abundant coat is not particularly fine-textured and may be tricolored with either black, red, or orange as a base color.

Tyrolean Hound (Tiroler Bracke)

119 Styria is an Austrian region of mountains and hills, rich in fir forests, meadows, and vineyards, with an Alpine climate and severe winters. Styrian hunters therefore needed a dog with strong muscles and a lot of character, one which would relentlessly pursue game, whatever the altitude and weather conditions, and be able to withstand hard work and cold. So from the Hanoverian Schweisshund and the Wirehaired Istrian Hound came this rough, intelligent dog which was so good at every sort of work that it eventually left its provincial world to be appreciated all over Austria, and in Germany and Yugoslavia, in fact, everywhere that serious hunting takes place.

His height ranges between 16 and 19½ inches (40 and 50 cm.) and his average weight is 33 pounds (15 kg.). He has rough hair, a likeable face, clear eyes, which are yellow in color, and a tail ending in a brush. His coat is generally red or yellowish, and he sometimes has a white patch on his chest.

Wirehaired Styrian Mountain Hound

120 This is a rather pleasant looking little dog with upright ears, a pointed muzzle, and a red coat with golden highlights that makes it look like a cross between a Chow-Chow and a fox. Of all the northern spitzes (the German Great Spitz, the Keeshound, and the Lapponian Herder), the Finnish Spitz is the bravest and strongest. Moreover, he has an excellent character and is a loyal friend to man. He is considered to be Finland's national dog.

The Finnish Spitz specializes in pointing out birds by barking. This tactic has earned him the nickname of "Barking Bird Dog." He is also an excellent watchdog.

His height is around 17½ to 19½ inches (44,5 to 50 cm.). He has straight hair that is soft to the touch and resistant to the cold. But the puppies need a lot of attention up to the age of about one year. Otherwise they are likely to become ill frequently, living the hard life of the Finnish hunter.

Finnish Spitz

121 The Finnish Hound, a hunter of hare and fox, normally winters by the fire with his master, taking advantage of the nightless days of summer to take part in the long hunts. Called Suomenajokoira in Finland, he is a very distinctive dog, with his expressive head rigged out with ears that are set high and widen over the cheeks like large fins. He has slanting eyes with a gentle look about them, a very prominent black, turned-up nose, a convex forehead, strong jaws, and a nobly elongated muzzle. His tail is rather long, and in repose, he lowers it down to his hocks.

His height is 21½ to 24 inches (55 to 61 cm.) in males: 20 to 22 inches (50 to 56 cm.) in bitches. His body appears longer than it is high, but this does not give it a heavy look, since the elastic, springy gallop that characterizes him when hunting keeps him light in appearance.

The Finnish Hound's coat is dense and rough all over his body. It is black with red markings, although there may be white areas on the muzzle, neck, underside, and paws.

Finnish Hound

122 The standard of the Petit Bleu de Gascogne is practically the same as that of the Grand Bleu de Gascogne, but he has shorter lines, giving him a more homogeneous and cohesive shape. The height of the Grand Bleu is about $27\frac{1}{2}$ inches (70 cm.); that of the Petit Bleu ranges between 19 and $22\frac{1}{2}$ inches (48 and 57 cm.). However, the difference between the two cousins is most noticeable in the shape of their heads, that of the Petit Bleu being much more refined and noble. If the Grand Bleu is better adapted because of his size to hunting wolf, the Petit Bleu is a champion hunter of hare. The hare leaves only the most difficult to recognize spore behind it, yet the Petit Bleu is rarely deceived.

The color of his coat is a blue created by black speckling on a white background; but white with black patches and red markings on the head and limbs is allowed.

Petit Bleu de Gascogne

123 Like other regions of France, the department of Ariège has its local dog that, logically enough, bears the name of Ariégeois. An all-purpose hound, excellent both in the country and in the mountains, he unites the qualities of speed and intelligence in his work, a good sense of smell, a strong voice, liveliness, lightness, and a passion for hunting.

The result of a mixture of three different bloods — the Bleu de Gascogne, the Gascon Saintongeois and the Briquet — the Ariégois was, for a long time, considered a bastard variety of hound, or "half-blood." This prejudice and lack of respect have not given very good publicity to the Ariégeois, which has continued to do his duty as a domestic hound without being in demand in other regions of France or abroad.

Twenty-one-and-a-half to twenty-three-and-a-half inches (55 to 60 cm.) in height, with a fine-haired, thick, shiny coat, the Ariégeois has a white and black coat with red markings on his cheeks and above his eyes.

Ariégeois

124   This is a dog with an imposing head, long pendent ears, and a body that is more than twice as long as it is tall, over short, crooked legs. It is just this lack of proportion that allows him to get through the thickest bushes, just as the Dachshund is able to get down the holes made by its quarry.

   There are two varieties of the Artésien: the true Artésian, redeveloped in Flanders, and the Norman Basset, bred in Artois. The differences between them are negligible, and breeders of today cross the two sister varieties with excellent results. His height ranges between 10 and 14 inches (25,4 and 35,5 cm.) which means that there are Artésien Bassets that are very similar in appearance and height to the Dachshund and the Basset of Artois. His weight is around 50 pounds (22,5 kg.). The coat is short and smooth and is either tricolored in white, tawny, and orange, or bicolored in white and orange or white and hare gray. He has large, dark eyes that reflect courage and goodwill. Because of this, he is often included in the category of companion dog.

Artésien Basset

125 There are conflicting accounts of the origin of this relatively old breed, but one cannot deny that he descends from the Bleu de Gascogne. While the height of this ancestor approached $27\frac{1}{2}$ inches (70 cm.), the Basset reaches a height of only 12 to 15 inches (30,5 to 38 cm.). The unusual look that his stature gives him and his noble bearing show him to be part of a great breed. He is a lively, attentive, little dog, a good runner, with an outstanding sense of smell, even for a bloodhound. He may be used for both feathered and furred game, as he is immediately obedient to the commands of his master. His eyes have an expression of goodwill and sadness.

The Standard requires that he have short, thick hair, a tufted tail that is carried gaily, a large head elongated into an oval shape, wide, floppy ears, crooked forelegs, and well-defined nails protruding out of his large feet. The coat is white with large, black patches and small, fiery markings on the eyebrows. Sometimes there are also red markings on his feet.

Basset Bleu de Gascogne

126 This is one of the finest of the great French hunting dogs and is especially useful in hunting roebuck and boar, either in a pack or alone. He is very brave and exceptionally vigorous, particularly in the early hours of the hunt. He originated in Vendée from a crossing of a white St. Hubert with the white-fawn Italian Bloodhound. As time went on, the Basset Griffon Vendéen was perfected, becoming a dog of elongated structure with a height varying between $14\frac{3}{4}$ and $16\frac{1}{2}$ inches (38 to 42 cm.). He has a long, rough coat and whiskers that give him a comic appearance. The color of the coat may be different shades of fawn or grayish white, white and orange, white and black, white and gray, or white with red markings, or it may be tricolored in any of these colors.

The Basset Griffon Vendéen has also been well received as a pet because of his gentleness, his fine character, and his proud but friendly expression.

Basset Griffon Vendéen

127   The Basset Fauve de Bretagne is a breed that has remained confined to its native province of Brittany, seldom appearing in other regions of France. He descends from the Grand Griffon Fauve, from whom he inherits his noble carriage, his fine elongated head, the quality and color of his coat, his behavior, and his lively expression.

    While his ancestor measured 21 inches (53 cm.) in height, the Basset Fauve should not exceed 14 inches (35,5 cm.). It is not surprising, therefore, that it took breeders a long time and many crossings (the Basset Vendéen was especially used) to reduce the Grand Griffon Fauve by 8 inches (20 cm.) and still concentrate in the smaller dog the ability to hunt in every type of terrain. Yet this was just what was required in a province of heaths and hills, forests, and rolling valleys.

    Bretons also enjoy the Basset Fauve as a pet because of his gentleness and his endearing look. His hard, short, dense coat may be various shades of fauve or wheat gold. A white patch on the chest is allowed.

Basset Fauve de Bretagne

The Griffon Nivernais is a one hundred percent French pointer that resembles a small Italian Spinone. Fashionable in the department of Nièvre, at the time of Louis XIV, the Griffon suffered the fate of many breeds after the French Revolution: when the nobility disappeared, so did its dogs. Thus the Gris de Saint Louis, ancestor of the Griffon Nivernais became extinct. The Griffon was redeveloped later. The breed was officially recognized by French Clubs only a few years ago. The Griffon Nivernais is not a fast dog, but he is tough and tenacious when hunting, has a slender yet strong musculature, and is able to withstand water, cold, and heat. Although not a dog of extraordinary qualities, he is, nonetheless, worthy of interest.

As required by Standard, his height ranges between $19\frac{1}{2}$ and $23\frac{1}{2}$ inches (50 to 60 cm.). His bushy (but not curly) coat is gray blue or wolf gray, like that of his ancestor, the Gris de Saint Louis, or boar gray, or even gray black, with red markings on the cheeks and around the eyes.

Griffon Nivernais

129 The Harrier is a smaller edition of the Foxhound selectively bred from specimens of small size. No other dog can equal his ability in hunting down hare. He combines a faultless sense of smell with the speed of an athlete and an impressive vitality. He can run 16 miles (10 km.) at full speed without stopping. It is not rare for a hare that has been pursued by a Harrier to end up falling to the ground out of breath without the strength to run further. And as far as cunning is concerned, the Harrier is certainly not second to the hare. Recently, the Harrier has specialized, with excellent results, in hunting wolf.

This little bloodhound measures from 17 to 21½ inches (43 to 55 cm.). He has a compact body, perfect balance, the feet of a cat, a splendid voice, and a smooth coat that is basically white with black and orange patches. He often has large black markings over his entire upper body.

Harrier

130 The Beagle is the descendant of a centuries-old English breed, known and appreciated since the early Middle Ages and cherished by many English monarchs: among them, Henry VIII and, of course, Elizabeth I. Probably the result of a crossing between the Harrier and ancient English hounds, the Beagle has the pleasing appearance of a little Foxhound. In the sixteenth century his dimensions were even smaller, and hunters who referred to him as the "pocket Beagle," took him to the hunt in little baskets attached to their saddles.

The Beagle is a specialist in hunting hare, wild rabbit, pheasant, squirrel, and quail, and, with the minimum of training, can also hunt fox. He can be taught anything. In Australia, for example, he is used for hunting kangaroos, and in America, he has proved marvelous at catching fish directly from the water.

Of all hunting dogs, the Beagle has the most harmonious voice—a polyphonic bark, one might say. During the hunt, the cry of a pack of Beagles reaches the hunter like an echo of the hunting horn. The English speak of the "singing Beagle." Hunting with Beagles is like hare hunting to music.

Affectionate in character and merry in its movements, the Beagle has also become a pet. It adapts very well to the town, is small in size, very clean, does not cause any bother, moves gracefully, barks little, and has a pleasant face. Because of all of these qualities, during the fifties it was the favorite breed in the U.S.A., coming ahead of the Cocker Spaniel, which is saying a lot.

His height must not exceed 15 inches (38 cm.). There is also a miniature variety, the Elisabeth Beagle, which measures less than 13 inches (33 cm.). The Beagle has a very short, sleek, thick coat, though there is a rough-haired variety. He may be any true hound color.

Beagle

Favorite of Henry VIII & Elizabeth I

131 Described by the English as "the Bloodhound in sheep's clothing," the Otter Hound is the rough-haired cousin of the Bloodhound, and the otter is the prey at which he is particularly aimed. In the course of years of hunting this quarry, the Otter Hound has become used to spending unbelievably long periods of time in the water without ill effect. He is able to pick up, early in the morning, the scent of an otter that has spent the night in a river. Then with his harmonious baritone voice, he will alert the hunter that the animal is close by.

Although it is said that he was the issue of a crossing between the Wire Fox Terrier and the Harrier, it appears that through his veins there also runs the blood of another unidentified breed.

His height ranges between 24 and 27 inches (61 to 69 cm.), and his weight varies between 75 and 115 pounds (34 and 52,1 kg.). The permissible colors are gray, gray mixed with yellow, reddish, black and blue with fiery markings. He is very brave, resistant, and happy in the water, but can also become a good family pet, being particularly patient with children.

Otter Hound

Foremost among all of the hunting bassets, the Basset Hound is also the most popular. One could say that he is a dog of French origin, English selective breeding, and American development. It was the Americans who spread his fame throughout the world, thanks to excellent breeding kennels which have been able to meet the great demand everywhere for Bassets, especially in Europe. This dog, which is long, like a train, with large, dangling ears, a wrinkled forehead, and a melancholy expression, has, like the Fox Terrier, the Poodle, and the Cocker Spaniel, enjoyed an enormous vogue.

The fame of the Basset Hound goes back some centuries. It suffices to recall that Shakespeare said, in *A Midsummer Night's Dream*, that it has "ears which sweep away the morning dew." But its modern popularity dates from 1863, the year in which it was shown for the first time at the Paris dog show. The English Royal Family could not fail to be won by the Basset Hound's expression, and King Edward VII became one of the Basset's most earnest breeders. It was called the "Cyrano of dogs" because of its long nose, which gives it an exterior sadness, while its heart brims with poetry and delicacy.

The principal aptitude of the Basset Hound is hunting in open country and underground, in the lairs of its prey. It is used for searching out fox, opossum, pheasant, hare, wild rabbit, and squirrel. He is not very fast, but he is accurate and has a good sense of smell (in fact, only the Bloodhound has a better one). Effective and sure, he falls silently onto his prey.

The Basset Hound is also a delightful pet, particularly after the selective breeding done by the Americans. The charm of his expression is irresistible. No one who has known a Basset can ever forget his good disposition, the sincere friendship that shines in his eyes, and his ability to look both humorous and melancholy at the same time. Devoted to his master and friendly to children, he is virtually incapable of biting, and even his bark has a pleasant tone.

He has a sturdy frame, but his height should not exceed 14 inches (35,5 cm.). He has heavy feet which point outward, like Charlie Chaplin's, and a tail that is carried gaily. There are no precise rules about the color of his coat, but generally the predominant color is white with wide patches of chestnut, liver, and sand distributed regularly over his body, particularly on his head. His coat is smooth, but there is also a rough-haired variety. He should be given his food in a special raised bowl that is particularly designed so that his large, dangling, velvety ears do not fall into the soup.

Basset Hound

134 The origins of the Italian Hound lie far back in time. He was known to the ancient Egyptians as a racing dog and was described by Xenophon and Aristotle. In pictures of the dukes and princes of Savoy, Gonzaga, and Sforza on horseback preceded by beaters and surrounded by dozens of hunting dogs wagging their tails, the dogs bear a marked resemblance to the Standard for the Italian Hound.

With packs of these dogs, hunters set out after boar, fox, hare, and rabbit, with complete confidence in the dogs' infallible sense of smell. So keen is his sense of smell that the Italian Hound can follow the trail of a wild animal without ever losing him.

The breed was formed on a base of the Egyptian racing dog, probably with a contribution of Molossus blood. It came from a town on the Rhône, known in ancient Gaul as Ségugiens. It is not known today whether the town gave the dog his Italian name (Segugio) or vice versa. In any case, Italy is the breed's true fatherland.

A born hunter, lively and hardy, tenacious in following game for hours and hours, tireless, and good in any sort of terrain, the Italian Hound soon became very popular with hunters. Unfortunately, the purity of the breed has not always been maintained, and it is not unusual today to find mongrelized specimens in the Italian countryside. Skilled breeders, however, continue to produce Italian Hounds of indisputable purity, as witnessed by those entered in dog shows.

The Italian Hound is a quiet, even-tempered dog who doesn't bite. He can sleep under a porch or outside in a kennel.

His ideal height is 21½ inches (55 cm.). His weight may vary from 39½ to 55 pounds (18 to 25 kg.). Bitches are slightly smaller. He has pendent ears and a long pointed tail. As with most hounds, there are two varieties of the Italian Hound: the shorthaired and the rough-haired (in the case of the rough-haired variety, the hair must not be more than two inches (5 cm.) long). The coat may be red, fawn, hazelnut with white patches, reddish black, or tricolor.

Italian Hound

Wirehaired Italian Hound

Shorthaired
Italian Hound

According to some dog fanciers, the Cirneco dell'Etna was first brought to Sicily by the Phoenicians. He looked at that time like a heavy greyhound, but the smaller space available to him, lack of food, crossings with various local dogs, the climate, and the terrain all contributed to a reduction in his size. In compensation, he developed a civilized nature and a new beauty. His name of Cirneco suggests that perhaps the original stock came from the coast of Cyrenaica. But then, to this African name was added that of the volcanic region of Etna on whose slopes he first learned to hunt.

As a hunter, he has the advantage of being able to approach wild animals noiselessly, so that his prey has no chance to flee.

In ancient Trinacria, people attributed the Cirneco with supernatural gifts. It was believed that he would attack anyone who approached a temple with sacrilegious intent, while giving a warm welcome to the devout. This sixth sense in addition to his abilities as a hunter earned the Cirneco high esteem, according to the Roman author Claudio Eliano.

The Cirneco has kept the classic lines of the Phoenician Greyhound, a look of lightness combined with a powerful bone structure. Proof against fatigue or changes in weather, he is an extremely lively, intelligent, loyal dog. From the thousands of generations which have gone before, he has inherited grace, wisdom, and calm.

Height: $19\frac{1}{2}$ inches (50 cm.). Maximum weight 31 pounds (14,2 kg.). Coat: light tan or sand.

Cirneco dell'Etna

137 The Podengo is the national hunting dog of Portugal and is a type of greyhound. There are three varieties: large, medium, and small, differing only in the height at the withers, which is 21½ to 27½ inches (55 to 70 cm.), 16 to 21½ inches (40 to 55 cm.), and 7 to 12 inches (17 to 30,5 cm.), respectively. He is an attentive and sensitive animal used mostly in hunting wild rabbit. His resemblance to the Cirneco dell'Etna is striking. Whereas the large- and medium-sized Podengos are also used as watchdogs in country houses, the Small Podengo is only used for hunting. Although he has the stature of a Dachshund, he is a well-proportioned dog, and his length is only slightly greater than his height. He is active and intelligent in hunting and has no need of any particular care: he eats little and voluntarily sleeps under the stars. The predominant colors for his short- or rough-haired coat are yellow and fawn, in various shades. He has extremely expressive ears that incline forward when he scents a rabbit.

Small Podengo

138 The Swedish breeder, Adolf P. Hamilton, gave his name to this dog that he created by crossing the Pointer with the Foxhound. From the Hanover Pointer, in particular, the Hamiltonstovare inherited an ability to withstand hard work, while from the Foxhound, he got his speed and sense of smell. From both, he took the ability to withstand cold and difficult terrain. His coat, which is normally rather thick, gets even thicker during the winter. Aesthetically, the Hamiltonstovare is a very pleasing dog with his black body, his tawny limbs and head, and his white chest. His head is noble: flat with a rectangular, very elongated muzzle and a conspicuous, black, turned-up nose with large nostrils. The height preferred by the Swedish Kennel Club is 22½ inches (57 cm.), and it must never exceed 23½ inches (60 cm.), nor go below 19½ inches (50 cm.). His eyes are brown and emanate goodwill and tranquillity. His ears are soft and pendent. His tail is set high and comes down to his hocks, getting thinner toward the end.

Hamiltonstovare

139 A descendant of the Dachshund, whom he resembles, the Drever has a long history, although the breed was only recognized twenty-six years ago. He is a small dog of comic appearance: long and muscular, with a nose that stands out against his white muzzle like the painted nose of a clown. Nonetheless, one would be very wrong to think of him as a toy. Despite his appearance, the Drever is, above all, a true hunter. He would much rather be hunting than playing indoors.

He is particularly good at routing out hare, fox, and wild boar. His impetuous courage leads him to confront even larger game, no matter how strong. And his baying is worthy of a much bigger dog.

His average height is 14 inches (35,5 cm.), but bitches can go down to even 12 inches (30,5 cm.). He has thick hair that lies close to his body. All colors are allowed, provided that white is included. He has lively, dark brown eyes, a long tail and a body with prominent bands of muscle. He is a common dog in Sweden, but little known in the rest of Europe.

Drever

140 The Swiss Hounds are, most certainly, among the breeds descended from dogs brought to the European continent by the Phoenicians before the Christian era. In Roman times these dogs spread to different countries. Over the centuries and down to the present day, the Swiss Hounds have remained pure in both appearance and character. Three handsome varieties are recognized today: the Bruno de Jura, which is black and red; the Bernese, which has a white coat marked with black and red; and the Lucerne, which is white flecked with gray and marked with red and yellow. The varieties are all governed by the same Standard and differ only in the color of their coats.

A twelfth-century fresco in the Cathedral in Zurich shows a pack of these venerable Swiss dogs pursuing a fawn; correspondence exchanged in the fifteenth century between the Sforzas and the writer Albrecht von Bonstetten also mentions their existence.

The Jura Hound, which gets its name from the mountainous Jura region in which it was perfected, is infallible when following and putting up game. While it is serene and affectionate in the home, it changes like a Dr. Jekyll when hunting, turning into an implacable adversary of wild animals such as deer, boar, or hare. Extremely lively and tireless, he is able to run with ease for an entire day over difficult terrain and in any weather, his ringing voice resounding through the valleys, urging the hunters to follow him and catch the prey.

Swiss Hounds have a height varying between 12 and 21 inches (30,5 to 53 cm.) and a weight of between $27\frac{1}{2}$ and 35 pounds (12,5 and 16 kg.). They are light dogs, but have a lot of muscle. Their ears are large and hang down. The tail reaches down to the hocks in repose. The muzzle is nobly elongated, and the coat is smooth. There exist smaller versions of the Swiss Hounds that are between 12 and 15 inches (30,5 to 38 cm.) high and have a pleasant Dachshund-like appearance.

Swiss Hounds

Jura Hound

Bernese Hound

Lucerne
Hound

143 In Yugoslavia, where game has not yet been indiscriminately destroyed, hunters are often accompanied by Istrian Hounds, with their snow white coats marked here and there with orange, their narrow, strong muzzles, and their steel-strong legs that allow them to withstand stony ground for hours and hours. The Istrian Hound's real speciality is the hare. He seems able to pick up its scent perfectly, while he is less interested in roebuck, fox, and birds.

The Istrian Hound can reach a height of 23 inches (58.5 cm.) and a weight of 44 pounds (20 kg.), 10 to 15 percent less in bitches. He has short but dense hair. There is also a variety with rough hair, about two to four inches (5 to 13 cm.) long, though never curly, and bushy eyebrows. He possesses all the same characteristics as his shorthaired brother, except that he may be somewhat heavier.

Smooth-Haired Istrian Hound

144 The Yugoslavs who are keen hunters also have good dogs. The Posavac Hound like all the Istrian, Balkan, and Bosnian hounds, and the Tricolored Hound, is very good at hunting hare and roebuck. He has an excellent sense of smell and does not tire easily. He is also a good barker, obedient, vigorous, and never holds back.

His height ranges between 18 and 23 inches (45 to 58,5 cm.), and his weight is around $39\frac{1}{2}$ pounds (18 kg.). He has a triangular, elongated head, a solid frame, a thick, stiff coat that is three quarters to one and three quarters inches (2 to 4 cm.) long, and a tail that is sometimes feathered and comes down to just above the hocks. The most common colors of the coat are reddish, all shades of corn yellow, and vivid tawny. There may be white patches, particularly on the chest and feet.

The Posavac is a dog of pleasant appearance, with lively eyes and an agile gait. He is a passionate hunter, but his use is practically confined to Yugoslavia.

Posavac Hound

The Rhodesian Ridgeback was bred by the Boers to be an ideal dog for Africa: able to bear the torrid heat of the day and the damp cold of the night, to go as long as twenty-four hours without drinking, and to be insensitive to insect bites. He is also called the African Lion Dog, and is effectively used against lions.

Outside Africa he is a domestic dog, calm, of a good disposition, and obedient. His Standard was fixed in 1822, in Rhodesia, from whence he gets his name. He is called Ridgeback because of the ridge down the center of his back where the hair grows in a direction opposite to that of the rest of his coat. This is the most distinguishing characteristic of the breed.

The Rhodesian Ridgeback is about 27 inches (69 cm.) tall and weighs a little less than 88 pounds (40 kg.). He is a strong, solid, and sturdy dog. He has a short, smooth coat in shades ranging from light wheat to red wheat, sometimes with a little white on the chest.

Rhodesian Ridgeback

Hunting Dogs:
Pointers and Setters

In the past, pointers were slow-moving dogs, who performed, without fail, the more mundane tasks of hunting. As long as hunting was only a matter of catching wild birds in a net or with the aid of a falcon, this primitive pointer was satisfactory. But when guns began to be used for hunting, it was clear that a faster, more eager, more energetic breed was needed. Thus around 1800, German breeders attempted to develop the desired animal by crossing the Italian Pointer with the English Pointer, though some authors insist that this crossing was spontaneous, occurring when the first English hunters came with their dogs to hunt in Germany.

The German Shorthaired of today is not only an excellent pointer, but he also excels in pursuit, in attacking predators, as a watchdog, and even as a bodyguard. He is a rustic but nonetheless distinguished-looking dog with an attractive chestnut and gray coat. He is affectionate, easy to train, has an earnest character, and is committed to his tasks.

His height should be 23 to 25 inches (58,5 to 63,5 cm.) with a weight of 55 to 70 pounds (25 to 32 kg.). It is to be noted that the lighter, more agile dogs can endure the activity of the hunt for longer periods. The hair of the German Shorthaired Pointer is thick, but short and soft to the touch. His tail is usually docked to one-third its length.

German Shorthaired Pointer

149 Sixty years ago, a small association of breeders developed this dignified and intelligent hunting dog from the German Shorthaired Pointer. Despite his excellent characteristics, he has remained almost exclusively within the borders of his home country, Germany. To the blood of the German Shorthaired was added the blood of the rough-coated Griffon, the Pointer, the Bloodhound, and the Airedale. From each breed, the new "Drahthaar" kept the best qualities : the sense of smell, the confident strength, the balance, the liveliness of temperament, the coat, and the harmonious lines.

About 24 to 26 inches (61 cm. to 66 cm.) tall, the Wirehaired has a brown coat, with or without markings, which makes him resemble his Shorthaired ancestor. He has a lively and aristocratic gait and is, above all, a dog for those who enjoy spectacular hunting. Working outside, he will freeze into a motionless point, assuming a sculptural pose with nose and tail raised. Very affectionate toward his master, he is jealous of other dogs on the hunt.

German Wirehaired Pointer

150 During the peaceful period of well-being that preceded the First World War, hunters in the rich province of Prussian Westphalia felt the need for a new hunting dog to replace the Brittany Spaniel which was, at that time, disappearing in the region.

In the capital of Münster, a town well known to historians because of the Peace of Westphalia, breeders began the process of developing such a dog by crossing the Spaniel and the Longhaired. Suspended in 1914, the work was resumed after the war. The perseverance and care of these German breeders was rewarded by the development of this fine breed, which is eager to hunt, good over all terrain and with all sorts of game, and capable of withstanding the cold and the damp.

His small size and his untiring willingness to work make the Münsterländer the ideal companion for modern hunters, who often travel about on motorbikes or in small cars. He has also proved himself to be a determined watchdog and an agreeable pet. His attractive looks

Münsterländer

Large Münsterländer

151 win him many friends. He has large ears covered with long hair, alert eyes, and a perky way of wagging his tail when he is happy. He is a distinctive-looking dog with a brown and white coat.

But his outstanding talent remains the hunt. Hunters appreciate the accuracy of his pointing, the precision of his retrieving, and the ease with which he adapts to working in the bush or in the water. Full of boldness in the face of any wild beast, he becomes truly ferocious when confronting birds of prey. More than once, the intervention of a Münsterländer has saved from a dire fate a fowl or lamb attacked by an eagle or a buzzard.

There are two varieties of Münsterländer, the small and the large. The only difference between them is size: 19 to 22 inches (48 to 56 cm.) and 23 to 24 inches (58,5 to 61 cm.), respectively. Where one stops the other begins.

Small Münsterländer

His beautiful lines and fringed coat may lead the observer to think that he is a dog with a German Shorthaired mother and a Setter father, but the origins of the German Longhaired Pointer are not entirely clear, and now that there are no good breeders of this dog, it is difficult to learn more.

In Germany, his birthplace and homeland, he is considered a dog of all work. He may be used against any small game of fur or feather, and he inspires confidence because of his excellent sense of smell, his innate obedience, the tenacity with which he hunts, and the calm that he shows, even at difficult moments. He is easy to train and works well with his master.

The Longhaired is a hardy, muscular dog with an aristocratic air. He reaches a height of 25 to 27 inches (63,5 to 69 cm.). His thick hair grows to two or two-and-a-half inches (5 to 6 cm.) on his flanks, neck, and abdomen and is tufted on his legs and tail, but it grows short and close over his head, accentuating his pure clean lines.

German Longhaired Pointer

153 Dog experts are not all in agreement about the origin of this breed. Did the Weimaraner come from the intentional crossing of a rare yellow pointer and a gundog carried out by Grand Duke Charles-Augustus of Weimar? Or is he a case of albinism in some ancient breed? And how was Van Dyck able to paint him just as he is today in a painting executed at the beginning of the seventeenth century? Whatever the answers, the Weimaraner is clearly an old breed that has always maintained the purity of its lines, thanks, no doubt, to breeders, but also to strong genetic characteristics that have neither changed nor weakened.

With a height of 25 to 27 inches (63,5 to 69 cm.), the Weimaraner is a dog with an excellent sense of smell. He displays a resolute aggressiveness when confronting wild animals (he was, at one time, used to fight bears), is an accurate hunter, and a perfect retriever, no matter what the terrain. He is a good-looking dog. He has a splendid head, and a coat that is a beautiful shade of silver gray, mouse gray, or buckskin. Because of this unusual coloration and his quiet ways, he has earned the nickname of ''the gray ghost.''

Weimaraner

The appearance of this gundog is unmistakable because of the prominent dewlap beneath his neck and his thick and slightly hanging lips. The Spanish hunters value this dog for his adaptability to all terrains and to bad weather, his acute sense of smell, and the ease with which he can be trained.

His body is strong boned and muscular, and the head is massive with pendent ears. He has a kind, somewhat melancholy, expression. His height is between 25 and 29 inches (63,5 to 74 cm.), with a weight of 55 to 66 pounds (25 to 30 kg.). The color of the coat may be white with dark brown spots or liver background with white spots.

Perdiguero de Burgos (Spanish Partridge Dog)

155 This dog, belonging to the greyhound family, comes from the island of Ibiza in the Balearic Islands, and resembles the Cirneco dell'Etna. He is a fast runner, but somewhat mischievous. He does not depend much on sight and hearing, relying almost totally on his sense of smell. Because of this, the Podenco is often used for night hunting. A quarter moon provides sufficient light for the Podenco to carry out his "nose-work" as if it were daylight, as he leaps surefootedly over streams and bushes. His favorite game are hare, rabbit, and roebuck.

His height is 23 to 25 inches (58,5 to 63,5 cm.) and his weight is around 48 pounds (22 kg.). His head is of a conical shape, with a coffee-colored nose that is very prominent. He has light eyes and a lively look. His ears are always pricked up. His hair is smooth and strong, his coat is uniformly white, red, or reddish yellow, or else, it is found in a two-color combination of white and red, or white and reddish yellow.

There are three varieties of Podenco: the smooth-haired (the most common type), the rough-haired, and the longhaired.

Podenco d'Ibiza

156   This is an old breed that was improved toward the end of the nineteenth century by the addition of blood of the Braque de Saint-German. While keeping his robust and muscular look, he inherited from this crossbreeding the distinction of being a great walking dog. Also called the Braque de Toulouse, he is the strongest of the French pointers. He has an independent, sometimes difficult temperament and needs good training and a master who knows how to dominate without intimidating. Under these conditions, the Braque d'Ariège (the name of his native region) can be an excellent pointer and retriever, good in all types of terrain and for all types of game. Like pointers such as the Saint-Germain, the Bleu d'Auvergne, the Dupuy, and the Bourbonnais, he is found all over France.

     Height: 23½ to 29½ inches (60 to 75 cm.). His Standard demands the following essential characteristics: a pink or light brown nose with flared nostrils, a docked tail, soft intelligent eyes, and a white coat with orange or chestnut patches.

Braque Ariégeois

157 This dog owes its fame to Napoleon. When the general occupied Malta in 1798, some of the knights who were stationed there disobeyed their order and went to France with their dogs. These were elegant, robust pointers, having dark brown coats with blue highlights.

In the Auvergne, a region characterized by volcanic soil, oak forests, pasture lands, and marshes, the dogs of the Maltese knights made themselves at home and quickly became among the most popular of the French pointers. Their acute sense of smell, their intelligence, elegance, docility, agility of movement, and endurance combine to justify their popularity. There is only one shortcoming which, however, many are willing to tolerate —the grip of the Braque Bleu d'Auvergne is a little too strong and therefore the plumage of the wild bird that he retrieves will be marred. The height of the Braque Bleu varies from 22 to 24 inches (56 to 61 cm.). His eyes are light chestnut in color and his long ears start low on his head. His tail is docked to six inches (15 cm.). His hair is short and somewhat soft.

Braque Bleu d'Auvergne

Although some authors hold that this pointer is indigenous to France, nearly all naturalists are agreed that all the shorthaired pointers are native to Italy and are the issue of a crossing between hounds and Molossus. Known for a long time as the Charles X Pointer, the French Pointer enjoyed a widespread popularity in France and England at the beginning of the twentieth century before being swamped by the wave of newer breeds. Nonetheless, he remains highly thought of today because of his excellent sense of smell, his solid point, his adaptability to difficult terrain, his loyalty, and his gentleness with his master. He refuses, however, to retrieve game from water, and his bite on the game he does retrieve is a bit strong. Impetuous during the hunt, he must be trained to display greater poise.

Height: 22 to 25½ inches (56 to 65 cm.). Weight: 55 to 70 pounds (25 to 32 kg.). He has light brown to gold eyes, and a fine white coat with large patches of chestnut. There is also a smaller variety that measures between 18½ and 22 inches (47 to 56 cm.). It has orange markings and is known as the Smaller French Pointer.

French Pointer

159 This ancient Magyar breed probably came from a crossing between the German Shorthaired and the Pointer, though today he bears slight physical resemblance to either. Nonetheless, the Hungarians claim that he has inherited their best hunting abilities. Apt as a pointer and retriever, the Vizsla is, above all, valued for his ability to hunt birds.

He is a sturdy, agile dog that measures between 22 and 24 inches (56 to 61 cm.). His coat is a delicate shade of dark yellow, which Hungarian breeders have succeeded in keeping pure without any markings. It has earned him the name "Yellow Pointer."

A near relative of the Vizsla is the Hungarian Longhaired Pointer. He descends from the Vizsla with the addition of German Wirehaired blood. He is strong and muscular, intelligent, and a very vigorous hunter in any terrain. All the Hungarian gundogs have an exceptionally fine sense of smell, cooperate well with the hunter, and are masterful retrievers.

Vizsla (Hungarian Pointer)

160   There is some dispute about the origin of this breed which its name does not help to clarify. Spaniel could mean Spanish, while Brittany defines him as being French. One possible hypothesis is that English hunters came to hunt in France, accompanied by their white- and orange-colored setters. By agreement among the hunters, these dogs were allowed to breed with the French hunting dogs, and this produced the first example of the Brittany Spaniel. The breed was recognized in 1907.

The Brittany Spaniel is an elegant, if thickset, dog. He is energetic, intelligent, and easy to train; and he quickly found a wide circle of admirers all over the world. Above all, his small size (17½ to 20½ inches (44,5 to 52 cm.) in height and 30 to 40 pounds (14 to 18,3 kg.) in weight) has made him the ideal dog for the hunter who lives in an apartment. He can be carried to the hunt on the back of a motorbike or in a small car. He functions well in any terrain, can endure the cold and the water, and prefers to hunt hare, partridge, and woodcock. He is indefatigable and lively, with his little stump of a tail always in motion. (Some dogs are born without tails.) If he makes a mistake, he must be reprimanded gently, because he is easily demoralized if beaten.

He has a fine, sometimes wavy coat that may be white and orange, white and chestnut, white and black, or tricolored. His nose is the same color as his coat; his eyes are slightly darker. His docility, restraint, and calm (the bitches are particularly good and tender mothers) qualify the Brittany Spaniel to spend his days alternating between the hunting field and the home. In the event that the dog becomes a pet, it is a good idea to regulate his diet and to take him for long daily walks in order to prevent his becoming fat.

Brittany Spaniel

161 The origins of the French Spaniel are as controversial as those of the Brittany Spaniel. Is the breed Spanish? Or did it develop directly in France with the contribution of the ancient Quail Pointer who may himself have had Spanish roots?

Be that as it may, in France the French Spaniel came into the hands of skillful breeders who made him into a dog of excellent character, strong and graceful, a passionate hunter but also docile. He is well known in France, while in the rest of Europe the Brittany Spaniel is preferred.

Not as tall as the other spaniels—his maximum height is 23 inches (60 cm.)—he has a well-developed musculature, an acute sense of smell and great endurance and versatility. He is always ready to search for and to pursue vigorously all types of game, whether fur or feathered.

His long tail is held low, and his hair is soft and, sometimes, wavy. The color of his coat is always white with chestnut-colored patches and smaller speckles on the legs.

French Spaniel

162 This is a variety of the French Spaniel. They share a common origin and resemble each other. The Picardy differs, however, in color. He is gray speckled with large chestnut-colored spots. He probably originated in the ancient French province of Picardy from which he takes his name. A strong and graceful dog, he is well adapted to the open plain as well as to marshland. He therefore specializes in the hunting of hare and wild duck.

Toward the end of the 1800s, the breed declined due to inbreeding allowed by the hunters. As a result of this, the Picardy Spaniel lost his beauty and his hunting abilities. However, skillful breeders were able to restore the breed to a new perfection at the beginning of our century.

The Picardy has a gentle and intelligent expression and sturdy limbs which tremble in the excitement of the hunt. His gait is lively; his tail is fringed; and his hair is thick and slightly wavy. His height varies between 22 and 24 inches (56 to 61 cm.). He has large feet and a light chestnut-colored nose.

Picardy Spaniel

163   The Pont-Audemere Spaniel differs from other breeds of spaniel because of the attractive tuft of hair which grows on the crown of his head and hangs down covering his long ears. It is reminiscent of the wigs worn by nobles of the seventeenth century. But this old-fashioned hairstyle conceals a vigorous, rustic, and indefatigable dog, well suited for hunting in difficult terrain. His name comes from a town on the river Aude in France. The Pont-Audemere Spaniel has been well trained for use in water, as well as for retrieving. In marshes he displays exceptional qualities, probably inherited from his progenitor the Irish Water Spaniel.

His height ranges between 20 and 22 inches (50 to 56 cm.). His prominent chestnut-colored nose fits well with the shape of his head, framed by its fringed ears. His hair is abundant, disheveled, and of a lustrous chestnut brown color with gray highlights. His eyes are mild and imploring. His tail is docked to one-third its length and is continually wagging.

Pont-Audemere Spaniel

The two breeds of the French Griffon each carry the name of the breeder who created them: Boulet, a French businessman, and the Dutchman E. K. Korthals, both working around 1872.

The soft-coated Boulet Griffon developed from an ancient Griffon that combined the blood of the Shepherd and the Poodle. He had, at first, a white coat. His breeder found, however, that because the coat was too visible during the hunt, it alerted the game. He therefore continued his breeding until he succeeded in developing a Griffon whose coat was the color of dead leaves and blended well with the autumn colors. It took ten years to perfect this amazing coat, but finally, a dog was created that was not only beautiful to look at but that also performed superbly in the woods and the marshes, was resistant to hot weather, was hardy, intelligent, and endowed with a fine sense of smell. Although not a fast dog, the Boulet Griffon is methodical.

His height is between 21 and 24 inches (53 to 61 cm.), and his average weight is 55 pounds (25 kg.). The Boulet Griffon is shaggy, with long but not curled hair, thick eyebrows that barely leave room for him to see, pendent ears, and a straight tail. He has a good nature and makes an ideal and faithful companion.

The Wirehaired Pointing Griffon, also called the Korthals Griffon, differs noticeably from his longhaired namesake, especially with regard to the quality of his coat, which is rough as boar bristle. He differs also in color (steel gray spotted with chestnut), in the eyes, which are not covered by eyebrows, and in the tail, which is docked to one-third. Korthals developed the breed in Germany and France with the blood of the Otter Hound, the setter, the pointer, and the spaniel.

Today, the Korthals Griffon is especially used for hunting quail and hare. He has a first-class sense of smell, and is energetic, enduring, and tenacious in the open as well as in marshland. He obeys the slightest gesture of his master and has an affectionate nature.

Griffon

Wirehaired Griffon (Korthals)

Softcoated Griffon (Boulet)

166   This very ancient dog is of uncertain origin. Some experts express the view that he was already known before the Christian era. Others say he originated in Russia, while still others believe that he came from the Piedmont, emigrating from there to France, where he became the progenitor of the French Griffon. This last contention, which would make him Italian, finds confirmation in a painting by Mantegna, in the Palazzo Ducale in Mantua, which shows a Spinone at the feet of the Duke.

    The Spinone flourished in the eighteenth century. He became the favorite dog of noblemen and commoners alike because of his strength, his endurance in the woods and marshes, his leathery skin, which permitted him to remain in the water for many hours, and also for the gentleness that is expressed in his affectionate, imploring eyes. Until the French Revolution, he was used in every way possible. Then came the wars, and the Spinone Italiano declined into almost total extinction. But toward the end of the nineteenth century the hunters began complaining, so breeders made use of the few acceptable dogs that remained and brought the breed slowly back into existence.

    Today the Spinone enjoys great popularity as an undemanding, patient, sociable, and intelligent animal. He swims well in cold water and is a perfect retriever. Between 24 and 28 inches (61 to 71 cm.) in height and 66 to 84 pounds (30 to 38 kg.) in weight, he is a sturdy dog with an elastic gait. His coat can be completely white, or white with orange- and chestnut-colored spots. The coat is dense and hard, lying close to the body, about two to three inches (5 to 7 cm.) in length, with a thorny quality from which he got his name: Spina means thorn in Italian.

    His tail is docked during the first months of his life so that its length will not exceed eight to ten inches (20 to 25,4 cm.) in the adult animal. Thanks to his sociable and affectionate nature, he adapts readily to family life in an apartment. During the summer, however, he needs several baths, and during the winter he must be taken for long runs.

Spinone Italiano

167   According to many dog experts, the oldest of the pointers is the Italian, a vigorous, well-proportioned dog. One finds his image in the Egypt of the Pharaohs. He is mentioned in the writings of the historians Pliny and Xenophone, and ancient Roman marbles show dogs closely resembling the Italian Pointer. Dante referred to him, and he is immortalized in a sculpture of Benvenuto Cellini which is now in the Louvre.

  The ideal companion for the nonspecialized hunter, the Italian Pointer is adaptable to any prey. He is an excellent discoverer of game, has a lively gait, is a calm dog, a reliable pointer, a faultless retriever, and has a vigorous appearance. Because of his gentleness, he is well suited to apartment life. He is affectionate and respectful and, when necessary, a good watchdog.

  His weight should be between 55 and 88 pounds (25 to 40 kg.). There are two types of Italian Pointers, differing only in the color of their coats: the white and orange and the chestnut roan. He has thick, short, shiny hair. The tail is docked to five to six inches (13 to 15 cm.).

Italian Pointer

The Portuguese Perdiguiero possesses Italian blood like other pointers; however, he has gained a very personal grace and style over centuries spent in Portugal. This is evident in his sense of smell, his tenacity in seeking out game, and his spectacular "point." According to the dog specialist Fiorone, this pointing behavior is always associated with a particular psychological state: face contracted, a fixed and ferocious stare, the head held immobile, the tail straightened out, and one leg lifted.

The Portuguese Perdiguiero has an average height of 22 inches (56 cm.), and the Standard allows for 2 inch (5 cm.) variation. The weight can range between 44 and 59 pounds (20 to 27 kg.).

This dog is not too fast, but he is persevering and silent in pursuit, tireless, and always entirely in accord with the hunter. He has a well-balanced gait, is lively, and is more sociable with humans than with his own kind. His coat is short and strong, and may be yellow or chestnut, either uniform or with markings.

Portuguese Perdiguiero (Portuguese Partridge Dog)

This pointer flourished during the second half of the nineteenth century and up to the beginning of the twentieth. During the First World War he gradually disappeared, and around 1920, there were only a very few survivors. These remaining animals, with the aid of German Pointers, were used not only to regenerate the breed, but also to improve it to meet the requirements of modern hunting. Above all, an animal faster in the pursuit of game was required.

The dog is medium in height, 24 to 26 inches (61 to 66 cm.) with a weight of 62 to 75 pounds (28 to 34 kg.). The coat is strong and coarse haired, about two to three inches (5 to 7 cm.) long. He has a thick skin that repels water, a muscular jaw, a beard, and a docked tail.

The Bohemian Pointer works well on every terrain, whether it is open land, woods, hilly countryside, or marshes. He works vigorously, but with an aristocratic style, following precisely the directions of his master. His performance in hunting is equal to that of any other pointer, and in Czechoslovakia he is widely used for hunting and is exported in large numbers.

Rough-Coated Bohemian Pointer

According to the best-known dog experts, the English Pointer derives from the Italian Pointer. For over two centuries, breeders added to the Italian Pointer's bloodlines the blood of the Foxhound, the Bull Terrier, the English Bulldog, the Greyhound, the Newfoundland, and the Setter. His name comes from the pose he assumes in order to show the presence of a wild animal.

The Pointer is so passionate a hunting dog that he has even been known to follow an unknown hunter carrying a rifle on his shoulder. Lack of discipline is never a problem. One of his chief characteristics is obedience to the orders of the hunter, even when it is not his master.

Giuseppe Solaro, an authority on dogs, has called the Pointer the gundog par excellence. He is a tireless runner with the lines of an agile athlete, an impetuous spirit with remarkable muscle tone. The Pointer combines the characteristics of strength and lightness. The speed of his gallop, his spectacular pointing, the eagerness in his eyes, and his outstanding sense of smell are all oriented toward the hunt for wild birds.

The Pointer works best in the open, where he runs at a great speed, smelling everything and signaling when he finds anything. He is especially popular in America, where there is much open space for hunting. The Pointer is immediately recognizable by his flawless carriage in point, nose up and tail held on the horizontal, as straight as a sword. His ears are soft and pendent. The skin is fine and reveals the venous network beneath; the coat is smooth and shiny without the slightest fringe of hair, and its colors are white and black, white and chestnut, or white with orange and black. His height is between 25 and 28 inches (63,5 to 71 cm.) and his weight between 55 and 75 pounds (25 to 34 kg.). The measurements of the European Pointer are smaller.

At the end of the hunting season, the Pointer is a welcome guest in the home, since he behaves like an aristocrat, is clean, and is patient with children.

Pointer

171 The English Setter owes his existence to an English shoemaker, Edward Laverack, who, thanks to a sizeable inheritance, was able to devote his life to his real passions: hunting and dogs. It is true that the first Setter (or a dog very similar) had already been developed in the sixteenth century in France with the blood of Spanish and French pointers. But it was Laverack who, in 1825, gave definitive shape to this very beautiful and astute animal who is today among the best known and most appreciated of hunting dogs. The work of Laverack was carried on and perfected by his friend Purcell Llewellin, and later, the Americans added a final touch. There is today a type of setter called the Llewellin Setter, which is very popular among skilled hunters.

The Setter got his name from the half-sitting position he assumes when pointing. One of the most beautiful among beautiful dogs, the English Setter has a finely chiseled head, and from there to his fringed tail, every line shows grace and strength. His sense of smell is exceptional, his play of movement is easy, and his body is tireless.

He can be used over any terrain. He shows the same enthusiasm whether in the open, the woods, or the water, and he can endure inclement weather as well as hot sun. This dog does not forget a lesson once learned, nor does he make the same mistake twice. Generally speaking, he is a dog for one person only, and one can see in his eyes his admiration for his master. He is very sensitive and his master must show him understanding and affection. He is also a good pet: always friendly and lively, with fast reflexes.

The height of the English Setter is about 25 inches (63,5 cm.). There are three varieties, differing only in the color of their coats: the Lemon Belton, which is white with orange spots; the Blue Belton, which is white with bluish spots; and the Liver Belton, which is white with chestnut-colored spots.

English Setter

Got it's name from 1/2 sitting he assumes when pointing

172   This fine Irish dog has a reddish chestnut coat, but at one time he was white with red spots, and it seems that he pre-dates his cousin the English Setter. The old and rare white examples are now highly prized. This dog has an unusually fine ability as a hunter: he is very fast with an ardent nature, great endurance, and an exceptional sense of smell. Moreover, he is an animal full of charm and grace. Because of his classical beauty and the color of his coat, he is also a popular pet. His temperament is somewhat changeable, however, and he possesses a spirit of independence. He requires a strong but wise hand to keep him in line.

   His ideal height is 27 inches (69 cm.), and his ideal weight is about 70 pounds (32 kg.). Dogs of average size are most agile and, therefore, the best for hunting. Like the Fox Terrier, the Irish Setter is long-lived: he can easily live for fifteen years.

Irish Setter

173   This dog differs from the English and Irish Setters not only in the color of his coat, which is black with mahogany-colored markings, but also because of his more robust body, thicker head, and shorter, silky and wavy hair.

His story is easily told. In the early 1800s, a Scottish duke, Alexander IV of Gordon, often borrowed from the farmers of the country some black and red dogs who showed a strange hunting instinct. One female in particular possessed an extraordinary sense of smell and was an infallible pointer. The Duke mated her with his setters and so began a new breed.

The Gordon Setter is not fast, but he is conscientious, even-tempered, a good swimmer, and tireless, no matter what the climate. He is also a fine watchdog and pet. He is fond of children and jealous of his family.

His height should be 24 to 27 inches (61 to 69 cm.) and his weight should be 55 to 80 pounds (25 to 36 kg.).

Gordon Setter

Hunting Dogs: Retrievers

176 Retrievers, as their name indicates, serve only to find the game shot down by the hunter and to retrieve it. The retriever may, therefore, be used either as an "assistant" to the pointer, with whom he usually develops a good working relationship, or alone, at the hunter's side.

The Curly-Coated Retriever was around 1850 one of the first breeds classified as a retriever. The breed developed from a cross between the Irish Water Spaniel, the Labrador, and the Poodle.

From head to tail he is covered with a thick mantle of curls that protect him against water and thorns. He is, therefore, suitable for any climate and terrain. Easily instructed, affectionate, and faithful, this retriever has many friends, specially in America and England.

His coat is black or dark chestnut. His height is between 21 and 25 inches (53 to 63,5 cm.) and his weight between 70 and 79 pounds (32 to 36 kg.).

Curly-Coated Retriever

177 Like his brother, the Curly-Coated Retriever, this dog will retrieve injured or dead game. He is particularly good at this task because of his exceptional sense of smell. If the Curly-Coated Retriever with his impermeable coat is better adapted for work in the marshes, the Smooth-Coated Retriever is trained to retrieve in the open, and excels in the woods, where the wounded bird can camouflage itself better.

He is a powerful-looking dog, with a tough musculature and strong jaws with which he is capable of carrying remarkable weights. He is also a good swimmer. His average height is 25 inches (63,5 cm.) and his weight not more than 70 pounds (32 kg.). Very popular until the early twentieth century, this breed has now given way somewhat to the Curly-Coated Retriever and the Labrador, which he resembles. At one time, these dogs had a tendency to bite, but modern breeding has improved them and the Smooth-Coated Retriever can now be considered a good pet.

Smooth-Coated Retriever

178   More than one hundred twenty years ago, Lord Tweedmouth returned from a trip to Russia with some dogs that had struck him by the beauty of their golden coats. By crossing them with the Bloodhound, he succeeded in reducing their size and sharpening their sense of smell. A graceful and lively dog was created, the most beautiful and distinctive of all the retrievers. The Golden Retriever is brave on land and works well in water. He can endure many hours of work beside the most demanding hunter without showing signs of fatigue. Of all the retrievers, the Golden is also the best companion dog.

    The Standard allows a height of 23 to 24 inches (58,5 to 61 cm.) and a weight of between 65 and 75 pounds (29,5 to 34 kg.). His muzzle is large and strong; the dark eyes convey intelligence; the coat is smooth and wavy; and the skin is water repellant. Since the most characteristic feature of the Golden Retriever is its distinctive color, tendencies toward the red or mahogany are not allowed.

Golden Retriever

179 This dog comes from Newfoundland, the island discovered by Cabot in 1497. It bears the name Labrador because the English fishermen who first brought him to Great Britain in 1800 came from the Canadian peninsula of Labrador. The dogs are robust, of good character, and excellent at retrieving anything from the water, whether it is a sheep that has accidently fallen into the water or nets torn away by the sea. Labradors are also good at retrieving game.

At one time, the Labrador was crossed with various other breeds and it has, therefore, helped to create new ones. But the true Labrador has remained pure in form, identical to the beautiful dogs who were imported by the English fishermen centuries ago. Today, he is still considered one of the best retrievers, especially for retrieving game from the water. He possesses an exceptional sense of smell and, like a true professional, will find wounded or dead game in any weather or terrain, even in marshes and lakes. The desolate and cold country of its origin has helped to make the breed strong and healthy. A very good swimmer, the Labrador has a short, rough, and thick coat that is impermeable to water and that protects him against ice. The Labrador is $22\frac{1}{2}$ to $24\frac{1}{2}$ inches (57 to 62 cm.) tall and weighs 60 to 75 pounds (27,3 to 34 kg.). He is not huge, but has a strong, solidly built body. He has large, expressive, mahogany or hazel-nut colored eyes. His ears hang down, well back on his head, the tail is thick at its base and tapers to a point, like an otter's tail. The coat may be one of two colors : either completely black or completely yellow. Spots or speckling are discouraged. While working, the Labrador is a serious and vigorous dog. In complete rapport with his master, he will respond to a whistle or a slight gesture of the hand. Due to his affectionate and docile character, he is a favorite pet.

Labrador

180   In 1807, an English brig coming from Newfoundland was stranded off the coast of Maryland. The crew and two Newfoundland dogs were rescued by the American ship Canton. The dogs adapted quickly to Maryland. They were brought on hunts and eventually mated with the local retrievers. The captain of the Canton himself reared the whelps along the Chesapeake Bay. Since they showed excellent ability at retrieving, they were called the Chesapeake Bay Retrievers.

Today the breed is strong, fearless, and resistant to cold and to water. When working in his preferred environment, the marshes, this dog is able to retrieve between two hundred and three hundred ducks a day. If he is taken along to the sea with the family, he will even play retriever with the children.

This lively, cheerful, and intelligent dog is 23 to 26 inches (58,5 to 63,5 cm.) in height and 65 to 75 pounds (29,5 to 34 kg.) in weight. His coat is absolutely waterproof. If he comes out of the water, not a single drop will remain after he shakes himself. His mantle is chestnut, light red, or straw colored.

Chesapeake Bay Retriever

Hunting Dogs: Spaniels

The name "Cocker" comes from woodcock. This spaniel is primarily a hunting dog and one of the best for flushing out woodcocks. He is active, tenacious, and moves skillfully through the bushes, flushing out the prey and bringing it under the fire of the hunter. Then he retrieves it in his delicate jaws and sets it at his master's feet. His excellent hunting abilities are combined with a love for man and for the home. He is an especially agreeable and affectionate pet. There is no dog more pleasant, more domestic, loving and lively than the Cocker, writes the dog expert Villard. His psychology is very interesting. He combines goodwill, intelligence, and mischief. His obedience is never servile, but is based on a perfect rapport with his master, whose intentions he devines.

He loves children and can be a good guard for them. He is active and tenacious. He will stay alone at home without barking and is serene and patient in his old age. In order for him to be quiet and obedient in maturity, he must be trained early and punished firmly and decisively. It should not be forgotten, however, that the Cocker is a sensitive dog and words are sufficent to make him understand. Blows are not necessary.

English Cocker Spaniel

183   The coat of the Cocker may appear in many colors, from tawny-red to orange, from lemon to black with brown highlights. His coat is smooth, silky, and curled. The tail should be docked during the first months of life. Too light a skeleton, a tail held too high, light-colored eyes and a kinky coat are considered faults. His ideal height is 16 to 17 inches (40,6 to 43 cm.) and 15 to 16 inches (38 to 40,6 cm.) for bitches. It is necessary to walk him frequently and to keep him on a balanced diet, since he has a tendency toward obesity.

184   This American variety derives from the English Cocker, but it is smaller, has a finer coat, and is more agile and more beautiful. While the English Cocker is still a hunter, the American Cocker is exclusively a house pet. He is an extremely sweet dog: happy, playful, healthy, poised, and neither nervous nor timid. He is a great friend to children.

His silky mantle, which may reach the ground, gives him a graceful and distinctive look, while his long ears complete the picture of a curious and delightful animal. His beautiful coat should be brushed thoroughly every day, and during the warm months, it is important to examine the ears for ticks or thorns that may lead to infections.

An American Cocker Spaniel should be 11 to 15 inches (28 to 38 cm.) in height, with a robust skeleton and an ability to run at a great speed. The most common color is black, but many others are permitted. This spaniel is a long-lived and strong dog.

American Cocker Spaniel

185 The Clumber is the most aristocratic of all the spaniels, not only because he comes from the French Kennels of the Duke of Noailles and the English Kennels of the Duke of Newcastle, but because of the long noble shape of his body, his quiet and dignified character, and his preferance for hunting only the choicest wild game, such as the pheasant.

At one time the Clumber was used in packs of eight to ten dogs, but today he works alone and has shown himself to be lively, precise, and intelligent.

He has a large head, ears fringed with long hair, a square nose, and deepset eyes. His body is long and Basset-like. The feet are round and hairy and the tail is short and horizontal. His weight is between 55 and 65 pounds (25 to 29,5 kg.). His coat is thick, silky, not curled, and generally white with lemon-colored spots or speckles.

Like all spaniels, the Clumber is appreciated as a pet because of both his friendly character and his unique shape and attractive coloring.

Clumber Spaniel

186 The Springer is a dog that has been known for so long that he is considered the founder of all the breeds of hunting spaniels. It appears certain that in the eighteenth century the American Indians used him for hunting on the prairies. But already a century earlier in Europe, the Springer had won the favor of hunters who hunted with nets and falcons. Later, when rifles were introduced, this spaniel was used mainly to find and retrieve game. The Springer Spaniel has a symmetrical shape, a compact and robust body, and an especially fine sense of smell. He is lively and cheerful, with his plumed tail constantly wagging.

The Springer's ideal shoulder height is 20 inches (50 cm.) and he should weigh between 49 and 55 pounds (22,2 to 25 kg.). He has a very thick coat which protects him in changeable climates. The breed comes in many colors but the preference is for white and liver, white and black, or either of these combinations highlighted with mahogany. There are completely liver or black Springers, but none are all white.

English Springer Spaniel

187 His shape is similar to the Clumber Spaniel's; an elongated body and short legs. His attractive outline often appeared in pictures of the nineteenth century, but he was only recognized officially in 1902.

Accustomed to life in Wales, with its difficult terrain and rough climate, the Welsh Springer Spaniel developed into a strong dog who could endure bad weather. (It is said that "for him it is always sunny.") He is an excellent retriever in ice-cold water and is capable of hunting for hours without tiring.

He has an independent character and must be trained well so that he will remain by the hunter's side. But he is a sensitive companion who loves company, especially that of children, and his little stump of a tail is always wagging. He measures 17 to 20 inches (43 to 50 cm.) in height. His coat is either a dark rich red and white or ivory white, with markings around the eyes and over the ears.

Welsh Springer Spaniel

188 As the name indicates, this spaniel is of Irish origin and specializes in working in the water. The breed was developed in the early 1800s from a cross between a Poodle and an Irish Setter. From the former, the Spaniel acquired the quality of his coat and his character; from the latter he inherited his strength and color. He specializes in wild duck. Therefore, he hunts mainly in marshes, where he remains lively and active even after many hours of intense work. His close, curly, waterproof coat protects him perfectly.

The Irish Water Spaniel is also a likeable family dog. His topknot, which makes him vaguely resemble an Afghan hound, his fine liver-colored coat, his exuberance, and his sharp intelligence have made him a favorite pet in Ireland, despite the difficulty of keeping his thick, curly coat in order. He has a strong elongated muzzle, small, alert eyes, and long, curly ears. His average height is 22 to 24 inches (56 to 61 cm.), and he weighs between 55 and 65 pounds (25 to 29,5 kg.).

Irish Water Spaniel

189 It took the English breeder Fuller nearly fifty years of experimentation to perfect this breed of spaniel. The breed was recognized in 1885.

The Sussex Spaniel is an energetic, tough, and eager dog, with a very fine nose. Normally he is quiet, cheerful, and serene. During the hunt, however, all of these qualities give way to the instinctive passion of the dog reliving ancient struggles. On the trail he barks continuously like a bloodhound and runs with a casual gait that is different from that of all other spaniels.

His coat is liver colored with gold highlights, a fact deplored by hunters, since the animal is easily camouflaged by the color of the countryside. In any case, the Sussex makes an excellent pet. His height is 15 to 16 inches (38 to 40 cm.), and he weighs 35 to 45 pounds (16 to 20,5 kg.). His tail is docked so that it measures 5 to 7 inches (13 to 17 cm.) in the adult animal. His thick coat has no curl, and there is a protective undercoat. His eyes have a gentle expression and his ears are not fringed.

Sussex Spaniel

Companion Dogs

192 Many owners of this extremely popular pet are not aware that the poodle was originally a hunting dog, and above all, a water retriever in ponds, rivers, and marshes. His French name "Caniche" comes from *canard* (*sauvage*), the wild ducks he brings back to dry land with such mastery.

The origins of the Poodle, which have been traced back to the beginning of the sixteenth century, are controversial. According to some, the breed first appeared in Germany, according to others, it was Denmark, France, or the Piedmont; but no bureau of vital statistics exists to confirm any of these theories. The most likely hypothesis is that he is descended from the Barbet, a breed of French hunting dog, now extinct. The Barbet was a large, rustic dog with a curly, woolly coat (black and white, dark gray, or white and chestnut) who was used to retrieve game in swampy areas. By a process of selection over a period of years, it is believed that the Barbet became the Poodle.

Besides being a useful hunter, the Poodle is a good watchdog and truffle dog. He often appears in circuses and variety shows as an acrobat and performer.

There are three varieties of Poodle: the Standard, which must be over 15 inches (38 cm.) at the highest point of the shoulders; the Miniature, which must measure more than 10 inches (25,4 cm.), but not more than 15 inches (38 cm.) at the shoulder; and the Toy, which measures less than 10 inches (25,4 cm.) tall. Some unscrupulous breeders reduce the size of Toy Poodles by giving the puppies alcoholic drinks that stunt their growth.

The Poodle, whether Standard, Miniature, or Toy, is a bold, intelligent, sensitive dog, easy to train and gentle with children. His natural grace is enhanced by the obligatory clipping. Recognized clips include the Puppy clip, the English Saddle clip, and the Continental clip. In the Puppy clip, only the face, throat, feet, and base of the tail are shaved. In the English Saddle and the Continental clips, further showing is done on the legs and hindquarters.

Poodles, regardless of size, may be black, chestnut, white, or gray. In America and England one also finds the colors blue and apricot.

When selecting a Poodle, it is advisable to look out for possible defects such as white nails, short ears, a curved nose, or missing or irregular teeth. The Poodle is born with a long tail that is usually docked by one-third.

A breed similar to the Poodle, the Portuguese Water Dog, has remained a hunter and is often used on fishing boats for retrieving objects from the sea, pulling cables to the shore, and courageously defending both house and boat.

Poodle

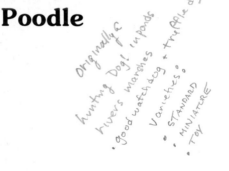

Toy Poodle

Standard Poodle

Miniature Poodle

According to dog experts, the Spitz may be the progenitor of all breeds of dog. Among fossils thousands of years old, skeletons of dogs have been found which bear a striking resemblance to the dog we now call the Spitz. There are many varieties of Spitz: in Italy there is the Volpino; in Germany, the Pomeranian; in England, the Pomerino; and in Holland, the Keeshound. All these varieties share enough common characteristics so that we may say we are speaking of a single family.

The Great Spitz is a German breed known for the beauty of its coat and the wide ruff that frames its sharp, foxlike muzzle. The four different colorations of the Great Spitz determine its variety:

1 The Wolf-Spitz—silver gray hair tipped with black
2 The Black Spitz—dark undercoat and skin
3 The White Spitz—a pure white coat with no yellowish tinge
4 The Chestnut Spitz—a coat of a single and completely uniform color.

The height of the Great Spitz varies between 16 and 18 inches (40 to 45 cm.), while the smaller variety should not be taller than 11 inches (28 cm.), with an ideal weight of 8.3 pounds (3,75 kg.). The small Spitz is primarily a house dog, but it possesses the same characteristics and even the same colors as the Great Spitz, having, in addition, an orange tone that is very popular. The Spitz is a lively, loyal, intelligent dog, with a loud bark. A good watchdog, he much prefers having the run of the apartment to being relegated to a terrace or corner.

The breed is strong and generally resistant to nasal infections, but like all members of the Spitz group, his intestines are a weak spot.

Great Spitz

195 Although this Spitz was developed in the Prussian province of Pomerania from which it got its name, it is considered by many as a dog without a homeland. Descended from the prehistoric *Canis palustris*, he was, for centuries, a guardian and a sheepdog and became a companion dog during the Renaissance.

He is an intelligent and lively dog, cheerful with his master, but with an alarming bark for strangers. He remains essentially a very obedient watchdog.

The Pomeranian has a very beautiful thick coat which may be either white or red without markings. He requires frequent grooming with a brush having short, hard bristles. The coat may be regarded as perfect around the age of three years. With age, areas of baldness may appear.

Pomeranians may range from 3 to 7 pounds (1,5 to 3,2 kg.). The ideal weight for show dogs is 4 to 5 pounds (1,8 to 2,25 kg.). The pups are born smaller and weaker than in other breeds.

Pomeranian

☆ got it's name from Prussian Province of Pomerania, Germany

There is no substantial difference between the Italian Volpino and the smaller varieties of Pomeranian. The eyes of the Volpino may be slightly larger and the skull a bit bigger, but these differences are not great enough for the dogs to be considered two different breeds. In some cases, however, the dogs can be distinguished by the color of their coats. The Italian Volpino should be either solidly white or red. The Pomeranian may also be gray, black, or orange.

The coat of the Volpino is long, abundant, and bristling and requires daily brushing. Baths, however, should be avoided, since they tend to soften and weaken the coat's consistency.

The Volpino, a dog of the working classes in eighteenth century Tuscany (the strain called the Volpino of Florence was especially popular with wagonners), rose quickly in social rank. He became a favorite of the nobility, and in Rome, was known for a long time as the dog of the Quirinal. He is now exclusively a pet: lively, exuberant, agile, and noisy.

The Volpino is 10½ to 12 inches (27 to 30,5 cm.) tall. His weight should not exceed 9 pounds (4 kg.). His tail curves back over his body nearly touching his neck. He should have triangular ears, bright eyes, and black nose and lips.

The breed resists infection well, and individuals may live fifteen years or longer. The Volpino is affectionate toward his master and devoted to the family, however, strangers may make him somewhat uneasy.

Italian Volpino

197 In 1960, Walt Disney's film *101 Dalmatians* brought unforeseen popularity to this unusual, sensitive, and friendly dog that had been overlooked for decades. Despite his name, no trace of him has been found in Dalmatia. He is a dog of very ancient origins. One finds him represented on ancient Egyptian bas-reliefs and on Greek friezes. He was not classified as a breed, however, until the eighteenth century when a very similar but now extinct breed, the Bengal gundog, was recognized in England. The Dalmatian was also known in medieval times as an undistinguished hunting dog.

On the other hand, the Dalmatian is distinguished by the fact that he will follow his master constantly, whether he is on foot, on horseback, or riding a bicycle. In 1800, in fact, he was known as the "promenade dog."

The Dalmatian is muscular, fast, tenacious, and an excellent guardian for the house, despite the fact that he is not a barker. He is versatile, intelligent, and easy to train and has been used with success as a sheep dog, a watchdog, and a performer in the circus. He is a faithful and amusing companion, but does not like to be treated severely. He has the asset of being, by nature, a clean dog.

The desired height for the Dalmatian is between 19 and 23 inches (48 to 58,5 cm.). He has short dense, shiny hair. His tail is sturdy but not long. It narrows to a point and is carried horizontally. The Dalmatian is white with well-defined black markings which should measure about an inch (2 to 3 cm.) in diameter on the body, and slightly less on the head, legs, and tail. There is also a variety with liver markings, but dogs with yellowish patches are not admissible in shows. The puppies are born white, chubby, and curious. The spots develop as they grow.

Dalmatian

198 The name Affenpinscher comes from the German "monkey-dog." To see how he acquired this name, one need only watch his comic behavior. He is of German origin, but neither his ancestry nor the exact date of his first appearance are known. It is assumed that he is related to the Schnauzer and the Belgian Griffon. He is, however, classed with the small terriers, with whom he shares numerous characteristics. Small, but well built, he is lively, intelligent, and a good watchdog. When a stranger enters the house he will break loose like a wild animal, but he restricts his aggressive behavior to intruders. In the family, he is affectionate, companionable, and pleasant.

His shoulder height should not exceed $10\frac{1}{4}$ inches (26 cm.) and all things being equal, smaller dogs are more valuable. Despite his small size, he is a hardy, fearless dog. His great enemy is the rat, and, good terrier that he is, he hunts him with decision and cunning. He has a small, stocky body, and straight legs and is completely covered with long, hard, thick hair that may be various shades of black, blue gray, or red. He has a round head, where hair forms thick moustaches and a thick beard and eyebrows. His eyes are large, round, dark, and very lively, and his pointed ears are set far apart. His tail, borne high, is covered by shorter hair than the rest of his body and is docked two-thirds. He prefers the freedom of the yard to the comforts of the house.

Affenpinscher

199 Pinscher meaning "biter" is a term used by dog experts. But this name does not do justice to the breed. In reality, the Pinscher is an affectionate, docile, devoted, and intelligent dog; it is only when guarding the house or car that he shows the ferocious side of his character and his sharp teeth.

The Pinscher's coat is short, dense, shiny, and uniform over his whole body, showing his strong musculature. Both the ears and the tail are docked in the very first months of life. His head is long and narrow; his eyes, dark and round; and his neck is slightly arched. The colors of his coat are black with mahogany patches, salt and pepper, or blue gray with markings that range from red to yellow. The height prescribed by his Standard is between $15\frac{3}{4}$ and 19 inches (40 to 48 cm.). In the miniature variety, a dog measuring more than $12\frac{1}{2}$ inches (31,75 cm.) or under 10 inches (25,4 cm.) is disqualified from showing.

Pinscher

The Germans call him Reh pinscher, *reh* meaning "doe," and indeed this small dog with his fine bones, erect ears, and shiny coat resembles that graceful animal of the woods. He is the miniature variety of the Pinscher, a guard dog bred as a show dog and companion. He has not, however, entirely forgotten his origins, and if put to the test, he will bark and defend the house like a professional guard dog.

Although his weight does not exceed 9 pounds (4 kg.), he is a sturdy dog and has a compact, harmonious, and muscular body. The colors of the Miniature Pinscher are black and tan, all yellow, reddish yellow, and chestnut. There is also a harlequin Pinscher, which has a light-colored mantle with black, gray, or reddish brown markings.

The Miniature Pinscher is a very sensitive dog who becomes extraordinarily attached to his master and enjoys playing with small children.

Miniature Pinscher

Miniature Pinscher with undocked ears

201 A descendant of the Manchester Terrier, the Toy Terrier is one of the smallest breeds. For a number of years toward the end of the eighteenth century, breeders amused themselves by mating the smallest animals, even those which might be considered dwarfs, in order to produce "toys" of smaller and smaller size. It was entertaining to play with these tiny creatures with their shiny coats, erect ears, and protruding dark eyes; and the "toys" were capable of attacking rats, even those larger than themselves. By reducing his size, however, the breeders had taken away the dog's physical resistance. He lost his ability to survive the colder months and became an eternal convalescent, needing constant care. The breeders decided, therefore, that the Toy Terrier should not weigh less than 5,5 lbs. (2,5 kgs.). Because of this decision, the breed has regained its popularity and the Toy Terrier has become, once again, a lively, healthy dog, despite his fragile appearance.

Toy Terrier

While his larger brothers are highly valued as guard dogs, the Miniature Schnauzer has become solely a fine companion dog. Indeed, he prefers to stay at home, lavishing all his attention on his master. This pleasant role, which he has taken upon himself, and his fine appearance do not however keep him from being a dog of energetic character, ever willing to bark at strangers and to make himself useful, be it in guarding his master's car or in catching rats.

His height should be between 12 and 14 inches (30,5 to 35,5 cm.). Signs of dwarfing are a serious fault. His coat is black or salt and pepper, and the hair rough. In the black variety, the hair may be a little softer. His thick eyebrows and frizzy beard give him the appearance of an "important person of small size."

Miniature Schnauzer

Miniature Schnauzer with undocked ears

203 The Schipperkee is native to Belgium and grew up in the houses of workmen, shoemakers, and boatmen. His name means "little skipper," in honor of Captain Renssens who developed and improved the breed.

In 1880, the anniversary of Belgium's independence, the Schipperkee was shown for the first time. Soon afterwards, Queen Marie Henriette acquired one, and the breed began to spread throughout the world. The Schipperkee was immediately popular in America as well as elsewhere. The most striking thing about him was his complete lack of a tail. There is a story that, two centuries ago, there was a cobbler who was envious of the Schipperkee belonging to one of his colleagues; so, with his leather knife he cut off the dog's tail. Surprisingly, the mutilation aroused enthusiasm instead of horror, and the association of Schipperkee breeders decreed that the tails of all whelps should be docked. Eventually, the first tailless examples were produced.

Looking like a much smaller edition of the Belgian Sheepdog, the Schipperkee is today a very brave watchdog, hardy, exuberant, an exceptional swimmer, and a quick learner. Despite his somewhat cool, detached expression, he has an inexhaustible affection for the family and especially for children. He has also been used in hunting, where he has shown himself to be particularly skillful in rousting rabbits and hares.

His face resembles the Spitz, with dark oval eyes, erect ears, and rough hair that grows longer around the neck. His coat is always black. There are three sizes of Schipperkee, weighing anywhere from 6½ to 18 pounds (3 to 8 kg.). The average Schipperkee will live fifteen to sixteen years.

Schipperkee

The Belgian Griffon, the Brussels Griffon, and the Brabancon are considered to be three varieties of the same breed. Their provenance is probably Belgium, although this is contested by the English, the Germans, and the Dutch. The breed was developed from crossings of the Yorkshire Terrier, the Affenpinscher, the Schnauzer, and the Pug. Thus, it is not unjustifiable that both the English and the Germans claim to have originated the breed. The first example appeared officially, however, at the Brussels exposition of 1880.

This pleasant dog received the name Griffon because he resembles the mythical Griffon, a monster, half eagle and half lion. Bearded and gnomelike, the Griffon can boast of neither the beauty nor nobility of his ancestors. In the early nineteenth century, Griffons were street and stable dogs, appreciated for their ability to quickly clear rats from infested areas. As time passed, however, thanks to his comic, almost human, expression, his intelligence, obedience, and sense of mischief, the breed won its place in the drawing rooms of the world. He was recognized as an ideal dog for an apartment, because of his small size and his abilities as a loyal watchdog.

A poet once described the Griffon thus: "Curious as a journalist, affectionate as a child, and enamored as a troubadour." Furthermore, he is easily taught and has received recognition in England at obedience competitions. Sometimes he even runs on his two hind legs, while waving the front legs like little arms. He is loveable, graceful, and as humorous as a clown. The first years of the twentieth century were a time of great popularity for the Griffon in France, Switzerland, England, and the United States as well as in Belgium.

He usually weighs between 8 and 10 pounds (3,6 to 4,5 kg.) and should never exceed 12 pounds (5,5 kg.). The Belgian and Brussels Griffons have extremely wiry coats that need stripping twice a year. The Belgian may be black, red and black, or black with mahogany patches. He has a large round head with a stiff ruff. His ears may either be cropped or left natural; they are carried semi-erect. The tail is docked by about two-thirds.

The Brussels Griffon has the same characteristics, except that his coat should be red with a little black around the muzzle. The Brabancon is also red, but has short hair that needs no stripping. In the United States, all three varieties are known as Brussels Griffon.

Griffon bitches often have trouble giving birth because of the size of the puppies' heads. It is often necessary to deliver the litter by cesarean section.

Belgian Griffon, Brussels Griffon, Brabancon

Belgian Griffon

Brabancon

Brussels Griffon

206　When the Roman legionnaires, under the command of Julius Caesar, landed in Britain, they found themselves fighting not only the fierce islanders, but also an unexpected enemy: terrifying and brutal dogs who would seize the calves of the invading soldiers in their strong jaws, these fighting dogs of two thousand years ago were the forefathers of the English Bulldog, a tenacious and surly dog that for several centuries kept his ferocious and bellicose temperament. The name Bulldog relates not only to the breed's plump aggressive appearance, so reminiscent of a young bull, but also to the power with which these dogs succeeded in combating bulls victoriously in the arena. Such combats were a popular diversion for the nobility from the beginning of the thirteenth century to the middle of the nineteenth century when they were prohibited by law.

After this, the Bulldog was threatened with extinction, but fortunately the porters and miners of Birmingham and Sheffield saved the breed. Through a long process of selection, breeders succeeded in giving him an even more frowning expression and a jaw that juts out in an exaggerated manner. It is for this reason that he can bite a bull and then cling to it until it is dragged down and yet go on breathing normally.

Although the Bulldog has kept his ancient physical characteristics ("beautiful in his ugliness," as one admirer described him), his character improved immensely until finally he could qualify as a pet. The modern Bulldog is a dignified and reserved animal, domesticated and protective toward children. He is faithful, intelligent, hardy, and clean. He almost never barks, travels well and is well behaved in the apartment.

The Bulldog weighs about 50 pounds (22,7 kg.). The bigger his head, the more he is prized. In any case, he is usually an expensive dog, partly because Bulldog puppies often must be delivered by cesarean section and partly because many bitches are sterile. The Bulldog is a long, low, compact dog with a massive head and flattened features. His ears should be set high, as far from the eyes and as wide apart as possible. The shape called "rose ear," which folds toward the outside, is most desirable. He has a large jutting chest, the chest of a gladiator. His shoulders and back legs are extremely strong. The front legs are somewhat lighter. He has a heavy tail that he should not be able to lift higher than his back. His coat is dense with fine, short hair. All colors are allowed except black and slate gray.

English Bulldog

207 The origin of this sweet-tempered dog is interesting. Both the French and the English claim paternity. The former claim that he is a native breed; the latter hold that he is a descendant of the English Bulldog. It remains an established fact, however, that around the middle of the nineteenth century, the French Bulldog virtually invaded Paris, especially in the working-class districts where there was hardly a coachman or butcher who did not own one. One of the most skillful breeders of the Bulldog, K. Hartenstain, a German, first saw one of these dogs in Paris during the Franco-Prussian War of 1871. It is known that during this siege the Parisians were forced to slaughter their domestic animals in order to survive. The fact that a Bulldog was left alive shows how much they cherished their "national breed."

Whether his origins are French or English, this dog is very different from the English Bulldog. He is small, compact, quiet, and even tempered—an appealing companion. The French call him the "favorite child." Yet he is, nonetheless, courageous, strong, and vigorous, a good guard dog and rat hunter.

He has a short muzzle with wrinkled skin, and when his lips are closed, his teeth should not show. He has "bat ears," muscular legs, and a soft, dense coat. There are two classes of French Bulldog: the lightweight, weighing under 22 pounds (10 kg.); and the heavyweight, weighing at least 22 pounds but no more than 28 pounds (10 to 12,7 kg.). It is important that he carry only the weight necessary for harmonious lines. Overweight animals run the risk of respiratory problems.

Permissible colors for the coat are "quail" gray (a white background with small speckled patches) or speckled black and tan with or without white patches on the chest.

French Bulldog

208   This graceful companion dog has been known since 1600. He lived in the houses of the nobility and the palaces of Kings, preferring the drawing room to the garden, petted by the ladies, and immortalized by the Court painters. One sees him in many of the canvases of Titian, Watteau, Rubens, and Van Dyck. Among his most famous masters and mistresses are Louis XIV, Madame de Pompadour, Marie Antoinette, and the Medicis. Although it is acknowledged that Italian breeders contributed greatly to perfecting the breed, the Continental Spaniel is considered today to be a French dog.

There are two varieties, which differ only in the position of the ears. One variety, the Phalene, has ears that hang down; the other, the Papillon, has, as its name suggests, ears poised like the wings of a butterfly. The two types are so close that both types of ears may be found in the same litter.

Even today, the Small Continental Spaniel is considered a dog of luxury. He should be combed daily, but baths are not advisable. Lively, graceful, intelligent, and spirited, he will leave his comfortable sofa to catch a mouse and will accomplish this feat with aristocratic style.

His coat is thick, shining, wavy, and lively to the touch. It only reaches its full splendor around the eighteenth month. It is longer around the neck, forming a veritable cape. There are no particular prescribed colors for his coat. Brown, red, yellow, bicolor, and tricolor are all admissible. According to the Standard, he may measure 8 to 10 inches (20 to 25,4 cm.) tall and weigh not more than 9 pounds (4 kg.). There exist, however, smaller varieties—veritable butterflies. Those who have owned these Papillon dogs say they make the best possible pets. They get on well with older people who spend long periods resting. They are very sensitive and love their masters to the point of self-sacrifice.

Small Continental Spaniel

Papillon

Phalène

Cousin to the Maltese, whom he resembles very much, the Bolognese is an ancient Italian breed that has been somewhat neglected. His origins are lost in the shadows of time. It is believed that the breed originated in Bologne, but when is not known. The first traces of the Bolognese elsewhere are around the year 1200. During the following centuries, he became a welcome guest in Italian and other European courts where he was especially appreciated by queens and noble ladies. The Gonzagas and Medicis bred Bologneses, and the Duke of Este once gave a pair to King Phillip II of Spain who declared that no other gift had ever given him so much pleasure. In more recent times, Bologneses were the inseparable companions of Catherine of Russia and of Madame de Pompadour. Many Renaissance paintings depict the Bolognese beside their aristocratic masters. In these paintings the dog is sometimes shown with dark markings on his white coat. Today, the breed has been carefully developed, and the Bolognese must be completely white without the least yellow discoloration.

He must not be less than 12 inches (30,5 cm.) tall and he should weigh over 9 pounds (4 kg.). Furthermore, his length should be equal to his height, so that he might be bounded by a square. Other than a slight difference in coat, this is the only characteristic which differentiates him from the more elongated Maltese. Both are classed as lapdogs.

The Bolognese is a delightful companion. He is affectionate, intelligent, playful, and deeply attached to his family. He will guard an apartment well. The splendor of his coat can only be maintained with daily care.

Bolognese

211 Some believe this breed originated on the island of Malta, others that he comes from Dalmatia. But in either case, the breed was developed in Italy, through crossings with spaniels and Miniature Poodles. The ''Bichon'' group, which is comprised of the Bolognese, the Maltese, and the Havanese, dates back, according to Darwin, to six thousand years before Christ. The first references we have to the breed, however, come from the Greek philosopher Theophrastos, who in 300 B.C. mentions in his writings a likeable dog of the ''Melita breed.'' Melita is the ancient name for Malta.

Handsome, intelligent, and curious, his most striking characteristic is his long white coat, which falls like a silk cloak, covering his legs completely. This coat requires daily care, for a ruffled and dirty Maltese loses eighty percent of his glamor. The tangles must be undone, then the coat should be brushed gently and combed, and finally a roguish topknot can be made with the long head-hair. The tail should curve over the back and be very bushy. The longer the coat, the more valuable the animal.

The Maltese is a sturdy and long-lived dog. He lives well in the open, provided it is not too cold. Acceptable size for showing: under 7 pounds (3,2 kg.) with 4 to 6 pounds (1,8 to 2,7 kg.) preferred. The nose must always be black. His eyes are large and slightly protruding.

Maltese

212 This breed is called *Canis Africanus*, but in reality, his country of origin is uncertain. He might be African, Asian, or American—no one knows. There are those who claim that he arrived in Mexico around 1600 from China. On the other hand, there is a probability that his country of origin is indeed Africa with its hot climate, since he is truly a hairless dog that requires, above all, high temperatures.

There is no other dog who so needs to be cradled on his master's knee. He is not tiny, weighing 11 to 13 pounds (5 to 6 kg.) and measuring up to 15¾ inches (40 cm.). But he has smooth, hairless, unprotected skin and trembles constantly, partly from the cold, and partly from nervousness. The few hairs he does have are on the top of his head. The color of his coat—if one can call it that—is elephant gray, sometimes veined with rose. He is a sensitive, affectionate, lively dog raised almost exclusively in Mexico.

Hairless Dog

213 Like the Hairless, this dog is completely without hair, but he is definitely of Mexican origin, and compared to the Hairless, he presents an even greater expanse of nudity, since he is 20 inches (50 cm.) tall. What the Chinese did with the Chow-Chow, so the Mexicans did to the Xoloitzcuintle: they ate him without needing to remove his coat. It was said that his meat was exquisite. This occurred despite the belief that he was the earthly representative of the god Xolotl, from whom he took his name.

The Xoloitzcuintle is cheerful and intelligent, but has a timid and reserved nature. He has a wrinkled skin, especially on the head and neck. The pups are born with the rosy color of piglets. They are lively and enterprising. They do not reach maturity until the age of one year.

There exists a miniature Xoloitzcuintle that is less than 12 inches (30,5 cm.) tall. He must be kept under blankets, even in the summer.

Mexican Hairless (Xoloitzcuintle)

This is the smallest dog in the world. He weighs, in general, only a little over 3 pounds (1,5 kg.), and some individuals only reach 2 pounds (900 gr.), a factor particularly prized in exhibitions. According to legend he originated in Mexico toward the end of the Aztec era, and indeed, he takes his name from a province of that country. Some paleontologists, however, argue that no dog existed in Mexico prior to the Spanish conquest. If this is true, then the most likely country of origin is China.

It is easy to think of the Chihuahua as merely a lapdog. But in spite of his fragile appearance, he is hardy, curious, courageous, and a good barker. He will stand up to dogs larger than himself (and all dogs are that). He is fond of alternating periods of rest with hunting for rats and squirrel. He is a playful dog, and like the terrier, he is possessed of a lively intelligence and quick reflexes. He is brave and loyal and will attach himself to one member of the family in particular and will defend him to the death.

The present Standard calls for a round head with lean cheeks and an accentuated nasal stop. The Chihuahua should have shiny, somewhat prominent eyes which may be black, chestnut, blue, or rusty red; large upright ears; and a tail long enough to be carried curved over his back. The colors of his coat may be fawn, chocolate, gray, silver, or cream and black, but mixtures are also accepted.

In general, litters consist of one or two pups. Deliveries are often difficult, and it is not unusual for the pups to be delivered by cesarean section.

Chihuahua

215 The leonine features of the Chow Chow appear in a hunting scene on a Chinese bas-relief two thousand years old. Of Chinese origin, he has been used as a guard dog on junks, a work dog pulling carts, and as a source of fur. Until a short while ago, the Chinese also used him for food.

Nineteenth century sailors returning from China with shiploads of oriental goods brought some of these attractive animals to Europe. Robust, noble, and fierce, they acquired the name Chow Chow from an English slang expression for Chinese curios or knick-knacks.

Toward the end of the nineteenth century in Europe and during the first years of the twentieth century in the United States, the Chow Chow enjoyed a period of great popularity. Still today, his proud and lordly appearance is admired in dog shows all over the world. The Chow Chow excels as a guard dog, a hunter of wolf, a draft animal (he is related to the Samoyed), and a pet. He is an animal of great beauty with an abundant thick, rough coat which may be black, tan, a metallic blue, or ivory. Colored markings are not permissible. He has small, dark, almond-shaped eyes, erect ears, and strong teeth. He is the only breed of dog whose tongue, palate, and gums are purple. His tail is carried curved over his back. He is about $19\frac{1}{2}$ inches (50 cm.) tall and weighs about 44 to $48\frac{1}{2}$ pounds (20 to 22 kg.).

Patient and understanding with his master and his master's children, he shows little interest in other people. He is strong and resistant to winter sicknesses. Clean by nature, he would rather suffer than soil the house. Although he suffers from the heat, shearing is not advised.

There exists also a shorthaired variety with the same Standard.

Chow Chow

The Pekingese is a small, unusual, and attractive dog with a flattened nose and soft ears. He can be traced back to 2000 B.C. when he was known as the "little lion-dog of Peking," because according to poetic legend, he was born from the union of a doting lion and a graceful squirrel. Chinese painting and sculpture of the Celestial Empire show him much as he is today. The Pekingese arrived in Europe over one hundred years ago when some English officers presented several of them to Queen Victoria. In 1860, when English and French soldiers plundered the Imperial Palace in Peking, they found a dozen or so of these dogs dead, killed by court officials so that they would not fall, living, into the hands of the ravagers. Several, however, managed to survive, and it was these that were given to the Queen and that began such an outstanding line.

The Pekingese is a small but sturdy dog, weighing not more than 14 pounds (6,4 kg.). He has a distinguished and airy bearing and a lively, intelligent expression. He is exclusively a companion dog. It is likely that over the centuries he has grown a bit proud and haughty, because there sometimes appears on his gnomelike features an expression of disdain (amusing in a dog). The Pekingese is affectionate and obedient toward the family; and although he is used to home life, he is not a timid dog.

The coat of the Pekingese must be long and straight, thick and soft, and never curly. It should be arranged daily with a light combing, and any tangles should be undone with the fingers coated lightly with Vaseline. In dog shows, all colors are admitted except platinum and liver. The nose is short with wide, black nostrils, the legs are short and the plumed tail curls back.

Pekingese

217 The popularity of the Pug has, over the last four centuries, had its ups and downs. Ladies of the eighteenth and nineteenth centuries liked to keep Pugs, convinced that against the dog's ugliness, their own beauty would stand out. Among his less attractive features, the Pug has the short and noisy breath of an asthmatic, and he is liable to grow fat and to develop an irascible temperament. His loyalty and friendship are, however, limitless, and he will dedicate himself totally to his master. Amiable with his friends and exuberant in nature, he needs little care.

Related to the Pekingese, but with a short, thick, shiny coat, he was most certainly brought over from China by the Dutch merchants of the East India Company. He soon became a favorite with Dutch, French, Italian, and English nobility. He received his French name "Carlin" in the eighteenth century, after a famous actor of the Commedia dell' Arte, Carlino, who was famous for his portrayal of Harlequin. Like the Pug, Harlequin wears a black mask. In German, he is known as Mops.

According to his Standard, the Pug should be *multum in parvo*, a lot of dog in a little animal. His ideal weight is from 14 to 18 pounds (6,4 to 8 kg.). He has a round, irregular muzzle with a short, pushed-in nose. He has a curly tail that rests on his haunches and pendent ears. Admissible coat colors are fawn (light, dark, or silvery), apricot yellow, and uniform black. A small mask is not a fault. A pet and house dog like his relative the Pekingese, the Pug needs affection and will return it. Above all, he needs a calm master who will not, through rough treatment, awaken his latent excitability. With the right master, he is truly a delightful dog.

Pug

Like the Pekingese, the Shih Tzu comes from the Celestial Empire of China. He is descended from the Lhasa Apso. Because of his resemblance to the sacred lion, he was revered by the Buddhist monks of Tibet. His name in Chinese means lion. He was brought to Europe for the first time in 1930 and, as is so often the case, was immediately taken up by English dog lovers and breeders.

The Shih Tzu should measure 9 to 10½ inches (23 to 27 cm.) at the withers, with some leeway allowed. Likewise, his ideal weight is 12 to 15 pounds (5,5 to 7 kg.), but he may vary 3 pounds (1,5 kg.) either way. He has a sumptuous coat with a thick beard, moustaches, and a heavy ruff. His eyes are large and dark, and do not protrude. His plumed tail is attached high and should be carried curled over his back. It is vital that he be brushed daily, and he may be given several baths as his hair dries quickly and perfectly. He is a dog with a lot of character—lively, gay, and good to all—and he carries himself proudly. His coat may be many colors, and white markings on his front parts and the tip of his tail are appreciated.

Shih Tzu

219 The Lhasa Apso, or "Abso Seng Kye" (Bark Lion Sentinel Dog), is probably the forefather of the Pekingese and the Shih Tzu. Because of his resemblance to the sacred lion, he was welcomed in the Buddist monasteries and villages around the holy city of Lhasa from which he takes his name. Since there are no lions in China, the Chinese painters made use of the Lhasa Apso as a model.

His coat partly obscures his eyes and his sight is therefore restricted; but this is compensated for by extremely fine hearing and sensitive skin, making the Lhasa Apso an extraordinarily diligent watchdog. In fact, in order to guarantee a night's sleep in their monasteries, it was the practice of Tibetan monks to leave the Tibetan Mastiff outside and keep the Lhasa Apso indoors.

His Standard allows for variable height around 10 or 11 inches (25,4 to 28 cm.). His body is longer than it is tall. He has a narrow head with a prominent nose. His hair is straight, long, and hard, not silky. The most prized colors for his coat are golden or lionlike colors. However, black, dark gray, or dark grizzle are allowed.

Lhasa Apso

220 The Tibetan Spaniel is a little companion dog with a proud and vivacious character. He is related to the Pekingese, the Pug, and the Japanese Spaniel. His origins cannot be traced. There was among emperors, ambassadors, monks, and travellers such a giving and taking of gift dogs that new varieties often appeared as one gift was crossed with another. It was in this way that the graceful Tibetan Spaniel was born. He resembles a Pekingese with a short coat, long paws, and a wide, plumed tail that curls over his back like a flag in the wind. His average weight is 22 to 23 pounds (10 to 10,5 kg.). He is cheerful and spirited, but slightly irritable with strangers.

The Tibetan Spaniel is born nearly hairless and remains so until the age of four months. Then the coat develops, eventually forming a double collar around the neck and shoulders. The colors of the coat may be gold, tawny, black, and reddish brown. Combinations of these colors are also admissible.

Tibetan Spaniel

221 From earliest times, the Japanese have always had great respect for dogs. They have sheltered strays and cared intelligently for valued breeds. The Chin, their most precious dog, is probably of Korean origin and is the only Japanese dog that is well known in the West. He was brought to the West for the first time in 1853 by a major who wished to bring a present to Queen Victoria. Since that time, the breed has taken root in England.

In Europe the standard for the Chin has been set at 8 to 12 inches (20 to 30,5 cm.) tall, with a weight of 6 pounds (2,7 kg.), but the smaller the Chin, the more he is valued. In Japan, they have managed to breed Chins so small they can be carried in a kimono sleeve. This is reminiscent of the art of bonsai, where trees are cultivated to remain small. But the technique of miniaturization always sacrifices the dog's health, and the Chin is especially susceptible to nasal infections.

The Chin has a thick coat, basically white dappled with black or red. He is an elegant dog, and his measured gait gives him the proud air of a little stallion. He is intelligent, devoted, and docile and extremely attached to his master, if a bit indifferent to what goes on around him.

Japanese Spaniel (Chin)

222 Until the mid 1800s the English Kennel Club classified four varieties of "toy" spaniel, which differed from one another only in color: the King Charles was black with tan highlights, the Ruby was red, the Prince Charles was multicolored, and the Blenheim was red and white. Today, the four varieties have been regrouped into a single classification bearing the name King Charles Spaniel. The name comes from the Stuart king, Charles II, who was often portrayed together with the dogs of this breed which he owned. The breed was also popular with other English kings, among them Henry VII.

The origins of these "oriental" animals is obscure. It is assumed that they are a combination of Japanese Spaniel, Pug, Maltese, and others. The King Charles has a large round head with a pronounced nasal stop. His eyes are large, his nose, black and shiny, and his tongue protrudes slightly from his jaw. His ears are long and fringed. He has a long, silky, wavy coat. His chest is broad and deep, his limbs, short and straight.

He is a graceful companion dog with a sweet face. He attaches himself immediately to anyone who pets him. The most prized color among the many which are admissible is black with tan markings on the muzzle, the chest, the paws, and under the tail.

King Charles Spaniel

223 The largest of the King Charles variety, this spaniel has been honored with the name "Cavalier." He has been developed relatively recently, and is in the process of conquering the hearts of lovers of "toy" spaniels. Presumably, this dog existed before King Charles lent him his name, but it is only recently that he has become popular. More sportive than his smaller cousins, he possesses a fine sense of smell, good eyes, and a strong jaw.

He is a lively dog with an instinct for hunting, an entertaining and graceful companion. His long, silky coat is not curly but is well fringed and may be black with tan markings, red, red and white, or tricolored. He has a more prominent nose than other "toy" spaniels. The tail is not docked by all breeders.

If one wishes to be precise, the Cavalier should weigh between $9\frac{4}{5}$ and $19\frac{2}{5}$ pounds (4,45 to 8,81 kg.).

Cavalier King Charles Spaniel

224 The Small English Terrier is also known as the Black and Tan Toy Terrier, a long name for so small a dog. He is a Manchester Terrier, reduced by breeding to the smallest possible size. This reduction in size, however, affected his health; and in the mid-nineteenth century, the puppies, which were often carried around in ladies' muffs, were usually delicate and sensitive to the cold. It was, therefore, decided that no terrier weighing less than 6 pounds (2,5 kg.) could be shown. As a result, the breed regained its stamina, and today, most individuals meet the standards of height and weight: 8 to 9½ inches (20 to 24 cm.) tall with a weight of 5½ to 8 pounds (2,5 to 3,6 kg.).

Needless to say, this little "toy" is a good companion, bright-eyed and intelligent, and always seeking the warmth of his master's hand. Should the occasion demand, however, he can also live up to his name of terrier. Despite his size, he is a great enemy of rats, which he fights with unexpected ferocity and skill.

His coat is smooth, shiny, and thick; his ears are erect. His bark would frighten no one. The two colors of his name should not shade into one another, but rather appear in well-defined patches.

Small English Terrier

225 In spite of the high social standing the Yorkshire Terrier has attained today, he is a dog of solid plebeian origins. He is named, it is true, after a famous English county, but he began as a rat catcher in local establishments, among workmen, millers, and miners. All this was around 1870, and since then, his rise in social status has met no obstacles. The breed probably developed by chance from crossings between such diverse dogs as the Skye Terrier, the Black and Tan Terrier, the Dandie Dinmont, and the Maltese. The result is a dog of singular beauty with long, silky hair, fine stamina, and great liveliness and intelligence.

During the period when he was hunting rats in the mines, the Yorkshire was taller then the present Standard. But careful breeding by the English has given him a height of between 8 and 10 inches (20 to 25,4 cm.) and a weight of between 4 and 7 pounds (1,8 to 3,2 kg.). His body is tiny, but well proportioned and compact. The color of his coat ranges from steel blue to red gold. At birth, the whelps are nearly black, and only at the age of eighteen months will the mantle develop its true color. The hair on the head is so profuse that it is necessary to gather it together with a ribbon. This prevents its getting into his food and allows him better sight. Besides, the gay ribbons are a fitting extension of his personality.

Although he has become a favorite of English nobility and American film stars, the Yorkshire has not forgotten his origins. When the occasion arises, he will throw himself furiously against his old enemy, the rat. In his small body he contains all the best features of the terrier: character, intelligence, liveliness, and gaiety. Although he is a good apartment dog, he prefers greater freedom. He suffers somewhat from the cold in winter, and should be protected with a woolen jacket.

Yorkshire Terrier

226 The Boston Terrier is one of the few really American dogs. The first examples of the breed were bred in Boston in the latter half of the nineteenth century. They were the result of a crossing between an English Bulldog and an English Terrier. These early dogs were known as Round Heads or Bull Terriers, and in 1889, a group of fanciers in the Boston area formed the American Bull Terrier Club to exhibit the new breed, which was eventually rechristened the Boston Terrier. Despite considerable opposition from Bull Terrier breeders, the Boston Terrier was recognized in 1893. Continued selective breeding involving a fair amount of inbreeding served to standardize the breed.

The modern Boston Terrier is a clean-cut, well-protected dog of dark brindle color with even, snow-white markings on his head, collar, breast, and legs. Black and white dogs are allowed, but are not as prized. He has a short head with dark soft eyes, strong limbs, and a body that resembles the terrier rather than the Bulldog. His tail is naturally short and should not be carried above the horizontal. His coat is short, smooth, and fine textured. The maximum weight allowed by his Standard is 25 pounds (11,3 kg.).

The Boston Terrier is an intelligent, lively dog with a gentle disposition that has earned him the title of "American gentleman." He makes an ideal pet. He is not a fighter, but if necessary, he can handle any situation.

Boston Terrier

Greyhounds

Ancient Egyptian tombs and Assyrian monuments show that the dog we call the English Greyhound existed four thousand years ago. Like the Deerhound, the Greyhound is an extremely fast dog of aristocratic bearing. It is almost as if his aerodynamic shape were designed in a laboratory to fit him for the pursuit of deer or wild boar. Anyone who owns a Greyhound knows he must not be allowed to run free, as he will attack chickens, cats, rabbits and other small domestic animals.

Toward the end of the sixteenth century, it became a popular sport to set Greyhounds in pursuit of hare. In the 1920s the sport flourished again, although this time a mechanical hare was used. Today, the majority of dog races use Greyhounds.

The Greyhound weighs from 65 to 70 pounds (29,5 to 32 kg.). He has muscular flanks, durable foot pads, and a long head with no stop. His eyes are large and his sight is sharp. His fine-haired coat may be black, red, white, blue, fawn, or brindle. He is a very intelligent, lively, courageous, and graceful dog. Yet, in spite of these gifts, he enjoys little favor as a companion dog. It is absolutely necessary for him to run unfettered over wide stretches of land, and this limits his adaptability to family life. Despite his apparent coldness, he is capable of great affection.

Greyhound

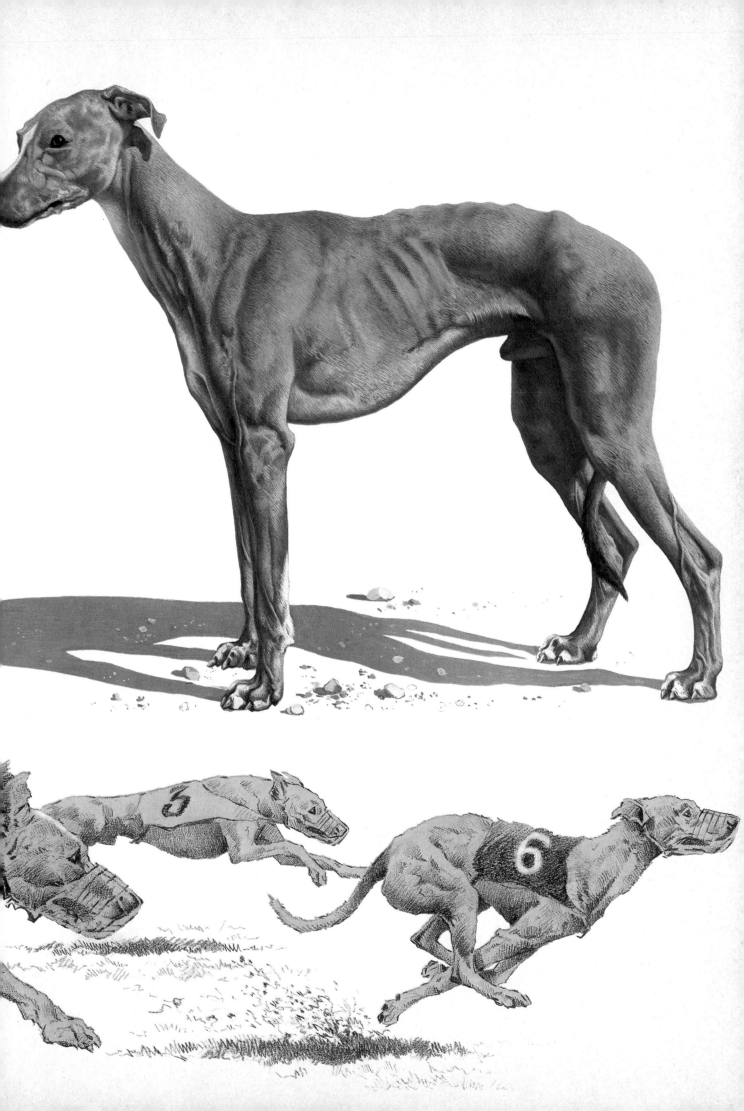

The origins of the Italian Greyhound are lost in time. The breed was brought by the Phoenicians to Egypt, and from Egypt it somehow came to Rome. Here the temperate climate helped the breed retain its ancestral appearance and even refine and perfect its classic lines. In Italy the dog developed into an intelligent, well-proportioned, friendly, and aristocratic animal. He became the companion of kings and noblemen and was to be found in all the courts of the Renaissance.

He was brought to America in the nineteenth century, where he became popular and was bred on a large scale. In Italy, however, he suffered a decline, and by the beginning of the twentieth century he had almost disappeared. However, there are today some important breeders of the Italian Greyhound in Italy.

The Italian Greyhound is a small, light animal with an elegant arched body. He possesses the characteristics common to all greyhounds, but with greater delicacy and more classic lines. He appears fragile, but is in reality a hardy dog. It is important, however, that he be raised carefully in hygenic conditions with plenty of fresh air and freedom. His ideal height is 13 to 15 inches (33 to 38 cm.) at the withers. He has a short and shiny coat that is extremely soft and of the same texture all over. It may be black, reddish yellow, or various shades of gray, but brindle coats and coats flecked with spots are not admissible. The eyes are dark, round, and expressive; the tail is long and thin and ends in a soft curve. The head becomes more pointed toward the nose, which is sharp and dark.

The Italian Greyhound adapts well to the family, especially if he is treated gently.

Italian Greyhound

231   The Whippet is a greyhound that has been bred with terrier and Small Italian Greyhound. He is smaller than the English Greyhound, but has kept many of its characteristics. Consequently, he is, by nature, a hunter of wild rabbit and, by adaptation, of mechanical rabbits, that is to say a racing dog. The Whippet is a dazzling animal who easily reaches speeds of forty miles per hour (65 kms.). Over distances of one hundred eighty meters he is the fastest dog in the world, so one can imagine the success he enjoys at the track.

     Affectionate, docile, and joyous, he is a fine companion dog. He adapts well to apartment life, provided that he can often run in the open country. A clean dog, his coat is free from smells and easy to look after. He is a good watchdog too, but will defend the house only by barking, not attacking. During the winter months he has to be protected against the cold, but nonetheless, he is a hardy dog and resistant to disease.

     The Whippet has a gracious and distinguished appearance and great muscular power. He must measure between 19 and 22 inches (48 to 56 cm.). A variation of half an inch (1,25 cm.) above or below these measurements will disqualify him in a show. All colors are permissible, either uniform or mixed. Among the most common are black, fawn, chamois, red, or any of these with white.

Whippet

232 The Deerhound first came to prominence in the Middle Ages. In the fifteenth century, Prince Edward II of York sang his praises in a book of poems. At that time, the possession of a Deerhound and his use for hunting deer was permitted only to those with at least the rank of Count. In the sixteenth century, the theft of a Deerhound set off a battle in which three Scottish nobles and a good number of soldiers on one side and about a hundred Picts on the other were killed. A nobleman condemned to death could buy his freedom with three Deerhounds.

The Deerhound is a hunting dog, particularly well suited to long hunts. He is an energetic dog who needs to be able to jump about and indulge in endless gallops. As the size of landed properties decreased in England, so his popularity declined. Today, however, he has found renewed favor, especially in the United States, Canada, and Australia, where there are still open spaces, and where he is used to hunt coyote and deer.

Adapted to country life, he is an affectionate and quiet dog and does not bite or quarrel with others of his breed.

His average height is 30 inches (76 cm.), and he should weigh between 86 and 106 pounds (39 to 48 kg.). His hair is rough and about four inches (10 cm.) long, a little longer on his head and throat. His coat may be gray blue or any shade of gray, even speckled, but it must never have white in it.

Deerhound

A dog very similar to the modern Irish Wolfhound was used by the Celts for hunting wolves. He was bred in Ireland and England and was brought to Rome by the legionnaires, where he was used to fight in the arena. His combat abilities were confirmed centuries later when a Wolfhound brought to Panama by Columbus on his fourth voyage to the New World was used by the soldiers to repel an attack on their garrison.

Today's Wolfhound has shown himself to be an excellent guard dog. He does not bite, but with his imposing size and bark he holds his victims at bay. If instructed to attack, he can kill a man.

His minimum height should be 32 inches (81,25 cm.) and his minimum weight 120 pounds (54,5 kg.). Dogs below these measurements are disqualified from shows.

Despite his size, the Irish Wolfhound has turned out to be a good, if somewhat cumbersome, companion dog. He requires at least a small yard, and during periods of hot weather, he should be allowed to run in the air.

His coat is long and rough all over his body and head, where it forms eyebrows and a beard similar to the Griffon. His coat may be gray, brindle, red, black, white, or tawny.

Irish Wolfhound

234   When the Moors invaded Spain in the Middle Ages, they brought with them a strikingly beautiful greyhound, the Sloughi. Bred with fine local hunting dogs, he soon became Spanish and became known as the Spanish Greyhound, or Galgo. He was used for hunting wild rabbit and hare, especially in the barren countryside of La Mancha and the moors of Alicante. Like a good greyhound he did all the work himself: rousting the game, chasing it, bringing it down, and carrying it to his master, who often did not have to use his weapons at all.

   Favored by the kings of Spain, he enjoyed a period of aristocratic splendor, careful breeding, and long hunts in packs. In more recent times the Galgo, like his cousin the English Greyhound, has descended to the dog tracks and has been adapted to the pursuit of mechanical hares. He has also been used successfully as a herd dog.

   Distinguished by his aristocratic shape and temperament, the Galgo has a fast and supple run, shiny dark eyes, a large and prominent nose, and folded ears. His back is arched, his legs are muscular with large flanks, and his long tail reaches to the ground. His shorthaired coat may be tawny with a black face, black, white and tawny, or brindled.

   Today these dogs are rare. One finds numerous Anglo-Spanish examples, but they resemble the English Greyhound more than the true Galgo. His height is 25½ to 27½ inches (65 to 70 cm.), and he weighs about 66 pounds (30 kg.). Bitches are slightly smaller.

Galgo (Spanish Greyhound)

235   The greyhound of the Balearic islands is also known as the Pharaoh Hound because he strongly resembles the greyhounds illustrated on the bas-reliefs and tombs of ancient Egypt. Presumably this dog was brought to Spain during some invasion, and then, isolated on the Balearic Islands, he survived unchanged over the centuries. Brought to the peninsula, he became the forefather of other Spanish breeds such as the Podenco and the Ibizan Podenco.

   A passionate hunter of hare and rabbit, he can also be trained to hunt birds. He is an elegant dog, a formidable jumper, and a fast runner. Nevertheless, as long as he has ample space to exercise, he is a fine house dog.

   The Pharaoh Hound is 25 to 27½ inches (63,5 to 70 cm.) tall. He has small, light eyes, a long, curved tail, and short, fine hair. His coat may be white marked with red or orange, or all red.

Pharaoh Hound

236 The Afghan is a very ancient breed. Legend has it that he was saved by Noah on his ark and was only thus able to survive to our times. In any case, the Afghan originated on the peninsula of Sinai, and several references to him have been found in an Egyptian papyrus more than four thousand years old. Only recently, in the twentieth century, was he brought to Europe, as Afghani breeders had always restrained his exportation.

Over the centuries, desert sheikhs kept the breed pure, and breeding has always been a serious matter.

Afghanistan is dry and mountainous country, and this regal dog lived with shepherds who trained him to watch the herds and to hunt gazelle, stag, fox, wolf, jackals, and leopards. The Afghan is a courageous dog, enduring in pursuit and indomitable in a fight. He is also endowed with a very fine sense of smell and a particular flat formation of foot that allows him to pursue his prey with ease, even in the most difficult, rocky terrain.

Afghan

237   In Europe, the Afghan is considered to be only an agreeable luxury dog, a sort of beautiful blonde, who is appreciated for his aesthetic qualities more than for his capabilities as a hunter. Perhaps this is because there are already so many hunting dogs in the West. He has become thoroughly bourgeois. · With his thick, soft coat hanging to the ground, he has been nicknamed the "hound in pyjamas."

Dogs should measure 27 inches (69 cm.), plus or minus an inch (2,5 cm.) ; bitches, 25 inches (63,5 cm.), plus or minus an inch (2,5 cm.). The dog should weigh around 60 pounds (27,3 kg.), and the bitch, around 50 pounds (22,5 kg.). All coat colors are admissible, but the preference is for cream to golden blond tones. The hair needs frequent brushing. An unkept Afghan loses much of his appeal.

Aloof and proud in appearance, he is affectionate but not expansive and is suspicious of strangers. He must be dealt with firmly, but at the same time sweetly, because he will rebel energetically at too harsh a scolding. He is a fast and tireless runner and has a characteristic elastic skipping pace. In spite of his thick coat, the Afghan stands the heat fairly well and is resistant to the bad effects of cold and rain.

238 Seluz, the ancient vanished Arab city has given its name to this splendid dog. For the desert sheikh, he was a gift from Allah, "as ancient as time, as fast as the fleeting instant," and since he was so beloved, the breed was kept pure through the centuries.

The Arabs used the Saluki, sometimes with the aid of a falcon, to catch antelope and gazelle. He is as clean a dog as Allah could wish for and will refuse to eat if his food is served in a dirty dish. In dog shows, it is sufficient to present him as he is without bathing him or fixing him up.

He is an affectionate and delicate dog, faithful and dignified, and still rare outside of the Middle East. It is likely that the Crusaders brought a few to Europe, but it was only at the end of the nineteenth century that Count von der Schulenberg, a member of the German legation in Teheran, really succeeded in importing Afghans to Europe. Today, the Saluki is bred in England.

Dogs should average between 23 and 28 inches (58,5 to 71 cm.) in height. Bitches may be considerably smaller. The Saluki has a thin graceful head, ears that fall like locks of hair, a long, flexible neck, and a tufted tail. His hair is soft and thick. The coat may be dark fawn, white, cream, brown, or red.

Saluki

239 The Borzoi is the most majestic, the most noble, and the strongest of the greyhounds. He must measure at least 28 inches (71 cm.) at the withers and may be much bigger. His weight is from 75 to 105 pounds (34 to 47,5 kg.).

His origins are obscure, but it is known that in 1600 a Russian Duke imported several Salukis from Arabia and crossed them with Collies. Over the following decades further modifications took place, the result of further breeding (with sled dogs from Lapland) and of the cold climate. The Borzoi was the favorite dog of the Tsar and was used for hunting wolf on the steppes. The Borzois, unleashed in a pack, set out as if a spring had been released. With curved spines, elongated necks, and outstretched ears, they galloped off at an incredible speed. The Borzoi is a courageous dog, strong and sure of himself. In the face of a Borzoi, a wolf is at a disadvantage. In more recent times he has been used in America to hunt wolf and coyote.

In Europe, the Borzoi (whose name means "fast") made his appearance in the second half of the nineteenth century, and Queen Victoria, as usual, was just in time to own one. Gaining popularity in England, Germany, France, Belgium, and Holland, he was bred as a companion dog, and was appreciated for his aristocratic character, his harmonious movements, his sculptured beauty, and his docility.

His long soft coat is wavy or falls in large curls. It may be pure white, white and orange, yellow, or gray. Black is less appreciated. He has an elongated head and muzzle, an arched nose, flexible ears, and long, flat flanks.

The modern domestic Borzoi has a gentle character and is peaceful and aloof. He seldom barks, and withstands both hot and cold weather well.

Borzoi (Russian Wolfhound)

The Dog From Birth To Old Age

The Dog From Birth To Old Age

Science has reached no agreement on the origins of the dog. The theories on this subject are so different that it is tempting for the dog lover to look on his friend as a gift from God to help man overcome his solitude. It is useless to wonder whether the dog descended from the wolf, the jackal, the coyote, or "Tomarctus." One day man simply found himself side by side with *Canis familiaris*. These early dogs were either wolflike, greyhoundlike, or foxlike. From their crossbreeding, three hundred different breeds have been created to date, and of these, at least two hundred now live in houses throughout the world. These breeds differ from one another in structure and behavior, but they have in common enough characteristics to be considered a homogeneous group in the eyes of science. In looking at the dog from the point of view of form, rather than behavior, one notes that these three hundred breeds differ from one another structurally to an extent unknown in any other family of animals.

Consider for a moment another animal who is also a good friend of man: the horse. Whether he is an Arab, a Tartar, a Maremma, or a valuable and carefully bred trotter, or even if we compare him with a mule, there will be differences in size, in musculature, in color, in the texture of his coat, and in the work or sport to which he is most suited; but his general structure, his overall look, will be significantly the same.

The dog, however, has evolved so many different variations of form, height, color, feet, ears, coat, and weight, that it would be easy to think of each breed as a different family from a different world. It is true that man has manipulated the dog to suit his pleasure, as if he were made of clay and needed only a breath to come alive. But the same type of manipulation has not produced the same kind of results with the horse, the cat, or the monkey. Scientific research has not yet discovered why by the game of breeding, it has been possible to develop breeds of dogs with such enormous differences from each other, differences on the order of those between the rabbit and the elephant. Man has not only changed the size of the dog, and his legs, and his coat, he has also changed his sensorial and behavioral characteristics to adapt him for work, for the hunt, for guard duty, or for the role of pet. He has succeeded in developing in each breed a unique pattern of attributes and aspects that is passed down perfectly by breeding from one generation to the next.

The dog was the first domestic animal in the world. It is alleged that he first appeared in Tibet at the same time as man and that he has lived in man's service ever since. The oldest monuments of the Egyptians, the Assyrians, the Babylonians, the Incas, the Mayas, the Arabs, the Chinese, the Greeks, the Macedonians, the Phoenicians, and the Romans have left us tangible evidence of the high regard in which this animal has always been held. He is pictured sometimes as sacred, sometimes as the embodiment of strength and elegance, and sometimes as the indispensable companion of man. Throughout the history of civilization, the dog has traveled step by step beside man, helping the hunter since the time of the caveman, following the Roman armies into battle, guarding medieval castles, taking part in the great hunts of Renaissance nobility, and adapting to the easier life of the nineteenth-century city. But until the nineteenth century, one could not really speak of well-defined, distinct breeds. It is true that in some isolated regions, in the great landholdings, and in the castles some breeds maintained their purity through the centuries. But throughout Europe, from the Dark Ages until the dawn of the nineteenth century, the mongrel triumphed.

In the nineteenth century, a more planned program of breeding was begun; in the twentieth century, official Standards have been fixed for the various breeds. Dog shows have been started where the best dogs of each breed are presented, and there has been an effort (perhaps not too successful) to teach people the necessity of ridding themselves of the plague of mongrels. These hardy, likeable, intelligent dogs are unfortunately, for the most part, doomed to a life of wandering and cruelty and are seldom lucky enough to find a master to save them from the gas chamber, vivisection, or the pound.

Purebred dogs are usually bought and, for this reason, have a value in the eyes of their owners which entails a certain respect for the dog's needs.

Pedigree

Modern breeds are classified with such precision and have such a variety of uses and personalities that they can fulfill all man's desires in all their nuances. Today, all civilized countries have associations for the control and development of different breeds.

The pedigree is an important document that gives the dog's ancestry for three or more generations and establishes the purity of his breeding. It also allows him to be shown in dog shows.

The most important American organization for fanciers of purebred dogs is the American Kennel Club, 51 Madison Avenue, New York, New York 10010.

Pedigreed dogs are registered with the American Kennel Club. In shows, they are examined by qualified judges for conformity to the Standard for their breeds. The road to the ultimate award, Best in Show, is a long one. Dogs are first shown in various classes: Puppy, Novice, American Bred, Bred by Exhibitor, and Open. The winners of these classes then compete against one another to determine Winners Dog and Winners Bitch. Depending on the number of dogs or bitches against which they have been competing and the popularity of their breed, the Winners Dog and Winners Bitch will be awarded points. They will also be judged against one another to determine Best of Winners. Any dog or bitch accumulating fifteen points and having two major wins (three- to five-point wins) under different judges is considered a Champion. Champions may enter Best of Breed classes in shows and on winning may compete for Best of Variety (Sporting Dogs, Hounds, Working Dogs, etc.). Finally, the winners of Best of Variety compete against each other for Best in Show.

Docking of Tail and Ears

For certain breeds, the Standard requires the docking of the tail and the ears. Originally, these operations were performed for purely utilitarian reasons and without aesthetic motive. Docked tails and ears offered no hold for another animal, such as a fox, during a fight. They also allowed more freedom of movement for the dog when hunting animals in underground lairs. Today, the docking is mainly a matter of beauty and fashion. It is obligatory for certain breeds, such as the Boxer, the Fox Terrier, the Doberman, and the Great Dane. Many dog owners, especially in England, however, do not have the tails and ears of their animals docked. Conducted under anesthetic by a veterinarian, docking is a relatively painless operation, and most dogs seem to endure it without ill effect. One should have the dog's tail and ears docked during the first months of life, because it is only in the third month, at the earliest, that the cartilage is strong enough to hold the ear in its proper position.

Depending on the breed, the dog's tail is described as long, short, thick, thin, fringed, tufted, straight, curved, and carried high or low. In some breeds, always for practiced and aesthetic reasons, the tail is totally or partially docked. The best-known breeds whose tails should be docked are various European hunting dogs, such as the German Shorthaired Pointer and the Breton Spaniel, various terriers, such as the Fox Terrier, the Airedale, and the Irish Terrier, as well as the Boxer, the Doberman, the Schnauzer, and the Poodle.

Standard

Naturally, there is no such thing as a perfect dog. What there is, is an ideal dog, constructed on paper by a man on the basis of the Standard. The Standard is the ensemble of the norms fixed for each breed by the club concerned with preserving the best characteristics of that breed and approved by the American Kennel Club. The Standard dictates the

244

dog's ideal height, his weight, the color and texture of his coat, his eyes, his ears, his legs, his tail, etc. This is why only a perfect drawing could bring together all the aesthetic details of a dog and recreate the marvelous, unreachable perfection of each breed. The Standard also specifies the dog's character and personality, and even the faults of the breed.

Legs

The Standard of dogs gives great importance to the legs. The front legs serve mainly to support the animal, while the back legs are for propulsion. The front legs may be straight, perpendicular to the ground, or irregular like those of the Bulldog, for example, whose front feet must be turned out. The back legs may be straight, forming a more or less acute angle with the ground.

In certain breeds of sheepdog, the Standard requires dewclaws (extra claws on the inside of the legs). In other breeds they are a disqualifying fault.

In order for the dog to develop sturdy legs, it is important that he receive the proper amounts of calcium and vitamins during his growing period. It is also important that when carrying a dog in one's arms, one avoids splaying his front legs. Also, the dog should have plenty of exercise in the fresh air and sunshine. In general, the height of a dog is measured from the withers to the ground. The withers is the point on four-legged animals immediately behind the neck—the highest point of the shoulders.

Coat

One characteristic which is always important in a breed's Standard is the coat. A dog's coat may be of one, two, or three colors. Certain breeds, such as the Mexican Hairless, have no hair and are pink in color. The hair of the coat may be short, smooth, hard, soft, straight, wavy, silky, or woolly. For certain breeds, such as the Wire Fox Terrier, a procedure called stripping is necessary. This consists of removing excess hair with the fingers or with a special serrated knife. Naturally, the dog should be stripped in accordance with the coat requirements of the Standard. For the majority of breeds, however, no special clipping of the coat is necessary.

Eyes

Dog's eyes vary according to breed. They may be round, almond shaped, protruding, deep set, and so forth. Most breeds have eyes that are some shade of brown. However, there are breeds with blue, black, yellow, amber, or red eyes.

It is a good idea to examine a dog's eyes frequently. If they are not clean, they should be wiped from the outside toward the nose with a piece of cotton dipped in lukewarm water or boric acid solution.

Ears

There are many different ear shapes, and the proper one for each breed is fixed by the Standard. They may be short or long, big or little, whole or cropped, attached low or high to the head, carried erect or hanging. The ears should be cleaned once a week with a piece of cotton dipped in a little mineral oil and wrapped around the index finger. Water should never be used. Even when bathing the dog, it is important to avoid getting water in his ears.

Nose

When one speaks of the nose of a dog, it is necessary to refer to two technical words used by breeders and judges, the *stop* and the *nose end*. The stop is the more-or-less accentuated indentation between the dog's eyes which divides the skull from the muzzle. The color of the nose end differs according to breed, but most dogs have black noses.

Heat

The birth of puppies is, first of all, dependent upon what is commonly known as the heat of the bitch. Normally the bitch comes into heat twice a year. The first heat will come at about eight or nine months of life, but possibly later, depending on the weather, the breed, the diet, and the season of birth. The beginning of heat can be recognized by a swelling of the bitch's vulva. This is almost always accompanied by small drops of blood. If the dog must be kept indoors, this is the time to protect carpets and furniture. The bitch can be fitted with a plastic belt with absorbent cotton, which is sold in various sizes in stores specializing in equipment for dogs.

Heat lasts for about eighteen days. During the first nine days, the period of bleeding, the bitch is not ready to be mated. It is during the second nine days that ovulation occurs and if mated, she may become pregnant.

If one does not want puppies, it is necessary to isolate the female during heat and take her only for short walks, always on a leash and with the protective belt. If one does want puppies, it is preferable to mate the bitch twice, with an interval of forty-eight hours between matings. One mating is usually not sufficient, and the second assures a better chance for the future birth of pups. After mating, one should allow the bitch to remain quiet for about twelve days, avoiding tiring exercise and long trips. In order to make the female less attractive to males, especially to those who come from afar, attracted by the smell of a bitch in heat, there are deodorizing products with a chlorophyll base available which are repulsive to male dogs. These may either be given orally or applied externally. Birth-control pills for dogs have not yet been perfected, and veterinarians advise against their use, since they merely serve to delay heat by ten or twelve days and may cause infections and metritis.

If the bitch shows undue interest in male dogs when she is not in heat, it is a symptom of nymphomania, a nervous condition that may be caused by genital infection. Male dogs, as everyone knows, feel the call of sex strongly, and it is best that their masters do not forget this. Young males may sometimes try to mount things or people, but a firm command and a light blow on the side should be sufficient to make them stop. Guide dogs for the blind are often spayed females who are thus sheltered from sexual temptations while performing their duties. Castration, or the removal of the testicles from the male, is a difficult and dangerous operation, since the testicles are connected in a complicated fashion with certain blood vessels. In cases of eczema, ulcer, or tumor of the scrotum, a veterinarian should decide if surgery is necessary.

Mating

In mating a bitch, it is a good idea to choose a time between December and March so that the puppies may be born and grow up during warm weather. Puppies born in autumn must, at an early age, endure the cold, the damp, and the inconveniences of winter. On the other hand, in larger breeds, puppies born in the fall tend to be stronger and more hardy.

It is possible to fertilize the bitch by artificial insemination. The puppies will be accepted for pedigree on the basis of a signed statement by the person performing the procedure. It is not a good idea to mate bitches during their first heats. It is much better to wait until after the third. The owner of the male is usually given pick of the litter when the puppies are weaned.

Gestation

The gestation period for dogs is about two months, varying from 58 to 65 days depending on breed, age, and number of puppies which will be born. If the birth is delayed beyond these limits, the bitch may be in danger and it is a good idea to notify a veterinarian.

The indications that a bitch is pregnant are lack of interest in males, ending of heat before the normal time, and swelling of the breasts. The most common sign, however, is the swelling of the abdomen, which becomes apparent toward the end of the first month.

When a bitch is expecting, it is important to follow several fundamental rules of hygiene: the necessary walks should not be too long or too active; food should be abundant but not excessive, with only a slight addition of meat; and finally, the drinking water should not be too cold. In the last month, one should avoid baths and limit the number of brushings. Cleanliness, quiet, exercise, fresh air, and good nourishment are the elements necessary to carry the gestation of the bitch to a successful conclusion. If everything goes normally, one should take the bitch to the veterinarian one month before whelping. He may prescribe a regimen of vitamins, calcium, and cod-liver oil. A second checkup should be scheduled about the fiftieth day of pregnancy.

Several days or several hours before the expected moment of whelping, the bitch will begin to prepare a bed for herself and her puppies and will show signs of agitation. This shows she is beginning to feel labor pains, which will come at shorter and shorter intervals. The breasts will be extremely swollen, and the abdomen will have the classic shape of the pregnant female. As the moment of whelping nears, the dog's temperature will drop from between 99.9° and 100.8° F. (38° to 38.5° C.) to between 98.1° and 99° F. (37° to 37.5° C.), and this may be considered a symptom of the impending birth.

Whelping

If all goes normally, the dog will need no help. Nonetheless, it is a good idea if someone close to the dog remains nearby to keep a discrete eye on things.

The puppies will be born one after another at intervals of about a quarter-hour. The mother takes care of everything. She frees them from the membrane, severs the umbilical cord, and places the puppies in a position where they will be comfortable and can reach her nipples.

Abnormal births may take the form of difficulty in expelling the fetus, either because of abnormal positioning, large size, or weak contractions. In these cases, one should get the help of a veterinarian.

Once the whelping is completed, leave the bitch quiet and warm on a clean bed. Strangers should not be allowed to go near her.

If one notices signs of weakness in the mother, give her a small spoonful of coffee. For two days she should be fed only broth and milk. Then nourishing food may be introduced. After several days, it is a good idea to have a veterinarian examine the puppies, prescribe for their needs, and give whatever advice is necessary for good growth.

In the days immediately before or after the birth, the bitch may experience mammary problems. The breasts will appear extremely swollen and painful and will secrete a yellowish gritty milk. These are symptoms of mastitis. It is a condition that should be taken care of immediately, because aside from being painful, it can lead to abscesses. It can be prevented by keeping the bedding especially neat and clean and paying special attention to the hair around the nipples. Mastitis can also result from the biting and scratching of the puppies. The condition will respond quickly to antibiotics, but the most common treatment is bathing the affected area with warm saltwater. Mammary tumors are not uncommon in older females. The only remedy for this is surgery.

Problems Caused by Whelping

The bitch may experience other problems after giving birth, such as the prolapse of the vagina or uterus. This can only be treated by a veterinarian. After a difficult birth or a miscarriage, there may be an inflammation of the uterus which is called metritis. This is treated with antibiotics and local irrigation. In order to prevent this condition, great care should be taken to keep the bedding clean before and after birth.

Miscarriage

A bitch may miscarry, though this is rare. The cause can be trauma brought on by fatigue, travel, a fall, blows, fear, cold, sickness, strong purgatives, or inappropriate medication. A natural miscarriage does not require any special care, though a visit to a veterinarian is necessary to be sure there is no danger of infection. Until recovery is complete, it is important to leave the dog quiet, give her good nourishment and keep her clean. It is not a good idea to mate her during the following heat.

Miscarriage may also be induced. This is often desired when the dog has mated with a mongrel or a dog of a different breed, or when no puppies are wanted. In order to induce miscarriage, it is necessary to give the bitch injections of estrogen between the fifth and fifteenth day of pregnancy. This will achieve the desired result, without discomfort to the bitch. In cases where the pregnancy is more advanced, induced miscarriages often cause infection, because the fetuses are not entirely expelled. This is why, in such cases, it is wiser not to intervene and to let the pregnancy come to term.

Delivery by Cesarean Section

Some dogs, especially smaller ones, do not have the strength to complete a normal delivery. In this case, a cesarean delivery must be performed by a veterinarian. This is a surgical precedure in which the puppies are removed through the abdomen. Bulldogs and Pekingese often have difficult deliveries. They are built with wide shoulders, and narrow flanks, so the front half of the pups is often too large to pass through the pelvis of the mother. A bitch can withstand two cesarean operations, but a third is not advisable.

Nursing

The puppies usually suckle for four or five weeks. Eight is ideal and ten the maximum. In this way, they receive adequate nourishment for growth. If the litter is large, the mother will run dry trying to feed all of them. Thus, it is important to pay particular care to her nourishment and to keep an eye on the condition of her breasts. When the puppies stop suckling for a bit, it is a good idea to wash the nipples with a saline solution.

When the puppies are fifteen days old, one may add to their diets a few spoonfuls of tea with several drops of lemon or orange juice and some vitamins. At the age of two months, they may be fed a regular diet of rice and chopped meat.

If the mother dies delivering the pups or does not have enough milk, the litter may be deprived of nourishment. The best solution is to find a nursing bitch who has only two or three puppies of her own. But, since that is an unusually lucky situation, it is wise to be prepared to nurse the puppies artificially with a baby bottle. During the first fifteen days, the puppies should each be given about 10 cc. of predigested skimmed milk (it can be found in pharmacies with instructions), six to seven times in twenty-four hours. If this is not available, use enriched milk made by beating a whole egg in $3\frac{1}{2}$ ounces (100 gm.) of milk. If one can find it, sheep's milk with added vitamins has proved excellent because it most closely approximates the milk of a dog.

If it is not possible to give the puppies calcium, one can add half a crushed egg shell to their meat or dog food for a month or two.

The dog is considered a puppy until about six months and an adolescent until the age of about twelve to eighteen months. The puppies should be seen by a veterinarian in their first weeks so that they can be vaccinated against distemper, leptospirosis, and viral hepatitis, all very serious diseases. If they are born during the winter, they should be kept in an atmosphere of 68° to 70° F. (20° to 21° C.) and protected from the damp. They are born with their eyes shut. The eyes open around the fourth day. A bitch may have up to sixteen puppies in a single litter, but it is preferable to allow her to nurse only ten, the number of nipples.

Buying a Dog

Anyone wishing to buy a dog should first take into account his own habits, his own character, the size of his house, and the type of family in which he lives. Quiet, methodical people, for example, should avoid the more active breeds. If one has use of a yard or a terrace, one may wish to choose a breed that is good as a watchdog or bodyguard. If one wishes to enter the world of dog showing, it is necessary to find a puppy of excellent breeding. If, on the other hand, one only wants a good and loyal friend, it is possible to get a mixed-breed dog free from many kennels.

Autumn and spring are the best seasons to buy a puppy, because the weather is good for taking them on regular walks. After about two months, the dog should be housebroken. Today, dog lovers seem to prefer small or medium-size breeds, which are easier to transport, eat less, and are better adapted to apartment living.

The best way to buy a dog is to go to a breeder. The habit of not putting money into a dog is still deep-rooted, since it is so easy to be given one by a friend. This is a mistake. When one buys a dog, one can demand that he be free of defects, healthy, and of good stock; since one has paid for him, one is likely to take better care of him than of a dog gotten for free. When buying a dog from a reputable kennel, one can be sure that care has been taken concerning his heredity, that is, the characteristics passed down from one generation to another. Since bad characteristics are as easily transmitted as good, breeders must be especially careful in the choice of mates. Moreover, there are no absolute rules governing the transmission of characteristics. A puppy may be just like his father, just like his mother, contain a little of each, or be a mixture of characteristics taken from his parents, his grand-parents, and his great-grandparents. Anyone wishing to buy a dog should see the parents of the animal himself and not trust unqualified incompetent, and even dishonest salespeople. In seeing a puppy's parents, one gets a general idea of what the dog will be like in the future.

If one does not wish to devote five or six months to training a dog, one should buy an adolescent dog instead of a puppy. The price will undoubtedly be higher, but the dog will already be trained and will have been given all the necessary vaccinations.

Male or female? The male is generally more impetuous, active, aggressive, and well built, while the female is more docile, more sensitive, and even more intelligent.

Dogs which are well suited to apartment living: Poodles, Terriers, Dachshunds, Cockers, Maltese, and in general, all small dogs. Medium or large dogs (Boxers, German Shepherds, Greyhounds, Airedales, etc.) need a terrace or at least a large balcony. For Setters, Pointers, and Griffons, among others, a yard is advisable, especially if their masters do not take them hunting regularly.

Feeding

A dog's life should run according to schedule both for his own good and for his master's. Normally, a dog is fed twice a day at the same time that the family eats. If he does not empty his plate in a half-hour at the most, it is a sign that he is not feeling well, and his food should be removed. There are those who prefer instead to give their dogs only one larger meal a day, late in the afternoon.

The digestive tract of the dog is short and can only handle small amounts of food at a time. It is not adapted to digesting coarse foods. Furthermore, the dog only chews his food slightly, and his digestion is slow. It is important, therefore, to give him food he can assimilate and to leave a sufficient interval between feedings. Dogs are best equipped to digest either raw or slightly cooked meat, but since they have lived with man for so many centuries, they can handle eggs, fish (white and without bones), milk, bread, well-cooked rice, pasta, vegetable oil, green vegetables, fruit, fresh cheese, bread soaked in bouillon, and crackers without hurting their digestion. On the other hand, one should never give a dog moldy cheeses, fried foods, cured meats and sausages, or sweets, except for a couple of dry biscuits given as a reward. In the diet of puppies, as has been said, the mother's milk is a complete food, having just the right balance of proteins, carbohy-drates, fat, and vitamins. It should, however, not be the only food. As early as possible, one should introduce broth and then progress to rice enriched with chopped meat.

Cooked meat or raw? The ancestors of our dogs ate raw meat, and it is a fact that it is still preferable today. The ideal diet for a dog consists of a bowl of rice (well cooked but not pasty) with green vegetables and salad vegetables, such as onions, radishes, and carrots. At the last minute, one should add raw meat to this, cut up in tiny cubes or ground. For the rice, one may substitute pasta or dry bread. And one may also use cooked meat, for example, table scraps, as long as it is cut up well and has no bones. Unlike their ancestors, dogs of today can lead full lives without ever tasting a bone. It is preferable not to give him any, rather than run the risk of fatal peritonitis. Chicken bones, above all, are absolutely prohibited, and one should be careful not to leave them where a dog might get hold of them. Some authors allow young dogs an occasional knuckle bone of beef, since he can chew on it without being able to swallow large portions.

Fish is a good food to give a dog occasionally and is indispensable in cases of eczema. Cod is especially good, but in any case, the fish should be boiled and all bones removed. For variety, one may also give the dog fresh cheese, though sharp or moldy cheeses are prohibited. Cheese which is high in protein, fat, and calcium has great nutritive value. It is also a good idea to accustom the dog to eating ripe fruit. Apples are especially good, and a small apple is useful in keeping the teeth clean. If the dog will eat them, he may be fed small amounts of leftover vegetables. Tomato juice or little bits of tomato are a good source of vitamins. Potatos, beans, peas, cabbage, and all mealy vegetables should, however, be avoided.

Naturally, dogs will gladly eat soups, broth with little pieces of meat, liver, or chicken. One should avoid, however, giving them too concentrated a mixture. One food which can never be overused is bread. Bread forms an integral part of a dog's diet, as it does for man. It contains essential food elements such as carbohydrates, salts, vitamins, albumin, and fats, and in combination with soup and chopped meat, it is very useful. The bread should be several days old, or, better yet, dried in the oven. This will make it easier to digest. It is even advisable to accustom the dog to eat bread alone, but this should only be done once in a while. This may prove especially conveninent on outings and trips. Dry bread stimulates salivation and firms the gums. Puppies should also be given stale bread; they can cut their teeth on the crusts.

Diet

It is not easy to establish the exact amount of food to feed a dog. This varies according to breed, size, age, season, and the type of life the dog leads. Some dogs consume a great number of calories, while others who consume much less, tend to get fat. According to a general, but useful, rule of thumb, one may say that for each 2.2 pounds (1 kg.) of weight, the adult dog needs 0.7 to 1 ounce (20 to 30 gr.) of meat a day. An animal weighing 22 pounds (10 kg.) for example, should eat a total of 7 to 10 ounces (200 to 300 gr.) of meat in his two daily meals. There is an erroneous belief that greedy dogs should be deprived of salt. On the contrary, sodium chloride becomes part of the bodily liquids and tissues, aids in digestion, and facilitates the functioning of the dog's organs. A normal amount of salt in the dog's meal is advisable.

The dog's food should be given to him lukewarm or at room temperature, never cold. If the food is kept refrigerated, it should be reheated for several minutes before giving it to the dog.

If the dog occasionally refuses to eat, don't force food on him. He knows how to regulate his diet better than we do. If he tries to eat, but cannot, it means there is something wrong with his teeth or his throat. Sometimes, when they have caught cold, dogs do not eat because they cannot smell their food. Hunting dogs who are not working keep the same hearty appetites, but to avoid them getting fat and falling ill, one should progressively cut down on their daily fare. If a dog has an abnormal appetite, trying to eat everything from dirt to pebbles to leather, or even fecal matter, there may be one of several causes. In puppies, it may be due to teething, or it may be caused by worms, lack of vitamins and minerals, or simply an insufficient diet. It may also be caused, however, by a malfunction of the pancreas, so it is a good idea to consult a veterinarian.

Dogs often try to swallow blades of grass when they are out in the fields or even on walks. This is healthy. It means that the dog, on his own, is adding vegetables to his meat diet.

It is better not to give a dog treats from the table when one is eating. But since ninety percent of dog owners do not have the strength to refuse their pets, it is at least important not to give them anything that might make them ill: no gravy or bread dipped in gravy, no bones, and no moldy cheeses.

Water

Obviously, the dog should be given water in a separate dish. It should be changed twice a day and always be available to the dog, especially on hot summer days and on returning from long walks. A few people put a small piece of sulfur in the dog's water, the idea being that the sulfur will act as a healthy disinfectant in the dog's intestinal tract. However, chemistry tells us that sulfur is not soluable in water, so this is a useless practice.

When the dog shows excessive thirst because of either indigestion, heat, or sickness, one should give him very weak unsweetened tea. Since dogs are not fond of tea, he will only drink when truly compelled by thirst and won't bloat himself needlessly with water.

Water accounts for sixty percent of the dog's makeup. He may lose half of his fat and proteins, but he will die if he loses ten percent of the water in his body. This is why the dog should always have available to him water that is fresh, but neither cold not hot; hot water may make him ill. On trips, it is a good idea to carry a bottle of water and a bowl.

Lack of Appetite

It happens occasionally that a dog will refuse to eat. Usually, lack of appetite is a secondary symptom of various illnesses, but it may be due to simple mistakes in the dog's diet. One should always try to diagnose and treat the illness that causes the dog to lose his appetite. If the lack of appetite is due to a poor or excessive diet, it is necessary to improve or cut down on the food given to the dog. In the meantime, one should give the dog the medicines necessary to normalize his appetite.

Indigestion

Indigestion in dogs, as in men, is due to overeating, especially of foods that are already indigestible. The stagnation of food in the stomach may be due to chills, dyspepsia (changes in digestion), and various gastrointestinal illnesses. Spoiled food, new foods, and hot foods can also cause indigestion. Being disturbed while eating may also prevent a dog from digesting his food. He may then show symptoms of indigestion such as lack of appetite, bad humor, pain, heavy salivation, and nervousness. One should allow such a sick animal to rest without food for twenty-four hours. One should also attempt to treat him with a purgative prescribed by a veterinarian. Sometimes the dog will vomit up the disturbing food spontaneously. In such cases, he should be given a light, bland diet for several days.

In cases of mild inflammation of the digestive tract and stubborn constipation, it is good to administer a laxative or mild purgative which will restore the normal functioning of the intestines. One may use Vaseline or olive oil (a spoonful mixed with the dog's food) as protectors and emollients. One may also use purgative mineral waters. In cases where it is necessary to empty out the intestines, one may have to use stronger purgatives such as salts or castor oil, but these must be administered in precisely the right dosages. For young dogs, a mild laxative is advisable. Mild cases of constipation may respond to use of glycerin suppositories, which may be cut in half for puppies. In order to avoid complications, always follow your veterinarian's instructions.

Emaciation

Emaciation in a dog may be caused by insufficient food or total privation, but it may also be a symptom of illness. When a dog becomes emaciated, yet retains his healthy appetite, it is necessary to have him examined by a veterinarian. Normally, with a diet rich in nutrients, with treatment of the sickness which caused the emaciation, and with various fortifying treatments, the dog will soon be back on his feet. If the dog is emaciated from hunger, it is necessary to build up his diet gradually, for it would be a grave mistake to stuff him.

Obesity

Most frequently, a dog becomes obese because his bodily organs accumulate fatty matter in greater quantities than is normal. This may be due to over-eating, lack of exercise, or a malfunctioning of the endocrine glands. Obese dogs become lazy, movement tires them, and they are subject to illnesses, digestive disorders, and eczemas. Bitches may become sterile or have difficult pregnancies. If the obesity is due to overfeeding, it will be sufficient to reduce the amount of food given and to eliminate fats and starches, giving the dog, instead, broth, vegetables, and meat that has been dipped briefly in boiling water. One should also take care to see that the dog gets plenty of exercise. In cases of obesity due to glandular disorders, it is necessary for a veterinarian to prescribe and oversee the treatment.

Bloating

Dogs are also subject to bloating of the stomach. It is particularly frequent in puppies that are weaned prematurely and fed on mealy foods. In cases of bloating, the belly becomes swollen and the back becomes concave. Such cases demand an immediate change to a balanced and moderate diet. The disorder may also afflict old dogs whose stomach muscles have become weak. In these cases, it is necessary to feed the dog four or five small meals a day instead of two larger ones and to limit his intake of water to brief drinks.

Anemia

Anemia is common in dogs. It shows up as a diminution of the quantity of blood or of certain of its parts. Primary anemia may be due to a natural pre-disposition of the dog's organism, insufficient diet, premature weaning, insufficient assimilation of nutrients, poor hygiene, too little exercise, or malfunctioning of the organisms responsible for the regeneration of the blood. Secondary anemia is caused by sickness or injury: internal or external hemorrhaging, high fevers and infections, gastroenteritis, nephritis, and parasitic conditions. The mucous membranes of an anemic dog will be pale and not red. He will be weak, without energy, apathetic, and easily tired. He will have a poor appetite, a weak pulse, irregular digestion, and he will become very thin. Anemia resulting from hemorrhaging is easily corrected. On the other hand, curing chronic anemia is a long and difficult process, and the help of a veterinarian is essential.

In order to restore the necessary amount of blood to the body once the cause of the anemia has been eliminated, good hygiene is indispensable. It is also important that the dog get outdoor exercise and a diet based on raw meat cut in little pieces, eggs, and milk. Raw or slightly cooked liver is also recommended. The veterinarian may further prescribe iron tonics, vitamins A and D, and hepatic extracts containing vitamin B12.

Rickets

Rickets is a growth disorder to which dogs are subject. It shows up especially in puppies as a lack of vitamin D, the vitamin which stabilizes calcium. It is characterized by insufficient calcification which results in the softening and deformation of the bones. Rickets may be caused by lack of calcium, phosphorus, and mineral salts in the diet, poor hygiene, lack of exercise, and exposure to the sun. Among the factors that may make a dog susceptible to rickets are poor digestion, serious infection, premature birth, and heredity. Rickets is only noticeable when it is already in an advanced stage. But if one treats it rapidly with calcium and phosphorus and a good diet, one may succeed in curing it. The best treatment, however, is preventive. Once the dog has been weaned, one must constantly keep his living quarters clean, give him a rich and varied diet which includes vitamins and minerals, and see that he has plenty of outdoor exercise.

Vitamins

Vitamins play a determining role in the development and health of the dog. Besides the vitamin complexes prescribed by the veterinarian, one should give the dog raw carrots, apples, apple peels, orange juice, grape juice, tomato juice, and avoid, as much as possible, overcooked foods. If one gives the dog a wholly meat diet, it is a good idea to add a dose of mineral salts containing calcium, phosphorus, potassium, magnesium, iron, zinc, manganese, and iodine. A veterinarian can prescribe the proper dosage. The sickness which results from a lack of vitamin C in the diet is scurvy. This may strike the dog at any age and shows itself by weakness of the capillary blood vessels of the skin. It may also produce swelling and ulceration of the gums, and sometimes anemia. The cure lies in a diet rich in vitamin C: raw liver, meat, milk, fresh fruits and vegetables, orange and tomato juices, and naturally, vitamin C.

Hygiene and Baths

By respecting the elementary rules of hygiene, one assures dog and master of a healthy peaceful life. This is why baths are a very important part of the dog's life. Opinions vary on the question of how often baths should be given, especially to puppies whose health may be affected. Many people feel it is unwise to bathe puppies younger than one year, and others feel that frequent baths have a detrimental affect on the animal's hair, which may lose its luster, and his skin, which may become dry from the loss of sebum. These people suggest giving fewer baths to rough-haired breeds and putting off the bathing of longhaired dogs as long as possible. Puppies should be given their first bath at the age of six months. But whether a puppy or an adult dog is to be bathed, the following precautions should be observed:
1 The water should be lukewarm, not hot.
2 Use neutral shampoos and soaps, not strong ones.
3 One should not soap the dog's coat directly, but should put some soap on one's hands and then begin lathering the dog at the tail and work toward the head.
4 Be careful to rinse the dog thoroughly with plenty of water.
5 After the bath, the dog should be carefully dried with an electric drier.
6 In order to assure a healthy reaction to the bath, one should see to it that the dog runs and plays afterward.

For dogs who are restless while being bathed, one should put cotton in their ears to prevent water and soap from getting in. The best time for the bath is in the evening, since the dog can then rest all night in a warm place. In the summer, on the other hand, one can bathe a dog in the sea or a river, if one is careful to see that he is dried by the sun. It is to be noted that black dogs should not spend too much time in the sun, because their coats run the risk of becoming oxygenated and turning reddish.

Also, there are products on the market for giving a dog a dry bath. The drawback to this is that the powders may clog the pores and inhibit perspiration.

Brushing

For all dogs, a good daily brushing with a hard-bristled brush is recommended. In this way, the dog will always be clean, and his coat will be shiny and alive. For longhaired dogs, brushing is indispensable. Besides keeping the dog clean, one avoids the mess of falling hair when the dog is shedding. For dogs whose skin has a bad odor, there are chlorophyll products available which can be applied in lieu of frequent baths. For certain skin diseases, the veterinarian will prescribe bathing the dog with medicines containing sulfur. In all large cities, there are salons where one may have one's dog bathed. They will also look after the dog's eyes and ears, cut his nails, and clip him artistically.

Apartment Life

Dogs, especially of small or medium size, thrive in cities and in apartments. For hunting dogs and large breeds who live in apartments, a daily walk of a half to one hour is absolutely essential, and all dogs need to be walked four times a day for hygienic reasons. It is important to housebreak a dog living in an apartment as early as possible and to teach him not to bark and to stay alone for several hours at a time. It is preferable that the dog does not sleep next to a radiator. When he comes in from a walk in the rain, he should be dried immediately.

Outdoor exercise is necessary for a dog. Dogs who live in the country or who have a yard to run in do not have the difficulties getting this exercise that a city dog may have. Life on a bed in the confines of an apartment will not do what exercise, fresh air, and sunshine will for the health of the dog, keeping his muscles active and stimulating all his bodily functions. Aside from the obligatory daily walks for purposes of sanitation, it is recommended that a city dog be taken for a long walk or run every day, or at least as often as possible. Watchdogs that are kept quiet indoors too long become fat and listless and lose their resistance to fatigue and sickness.

Bed and Kennel

It is a good rule that the dog should not be allowed to sleep in the bedroom (though there are exceptions). Instead, he should sleep in the kitchen, foyer, hall, covered terrace, or in a corner reserved for him. The place should always be the same, and he should have a cushion, small mattress, old coverlet, or piece of carpet to sleep on. This bed should be changed and washed periodically.

Small dogs can be housed happily in an apartment, where they may have their small beds or couch of rags. Watchdogs, guard dogs, and hunting dogs, on the other hand, may also sleep in the yard, in a store, or in a garage (in this last case, be careful of poisonous fumes from cars). The best place to construct an outdoor kennel is in a spot which is protected from the wind and wet. The little house should be big enough for the dog. He should be able to lie down in it comfortably and enter and leave it easily. The classic doghouse is made of wood. It should be varnished inside and out to protect it from the weather and to avoid the breeding of the larvae of parasites in the wood. Furthermore, it is a good idea to build a kennel that can be taken apart to facilitate periodic cleaning. Various manufacturers specialize in constructing functional kennels of wood, aluminium, or plastic.

There should be only one opening to the doghouse, and it should be big enough to permit the dog to come and go easily. During wet or windy weather and in the winter, it is a good idea to hang a heavy piece of cloth, such as an old coverlet, over the entrance to the kennel. This is the only way to protect the dog from dampness and the rheumatism it may cause. Finally, the kennel should be raised four inches (10 cm.) off the ground and should be covered with tar paper or a sheet of galvanized metal. After a rainy day, one should inspect the kennel to be sure no water has gotten in. For a bed, an old coverlet, which should be aired frequently, is sufficient. It is also satisfactory to make a small mattress of rags or wood chips, but never use straw because of the risk of parasites. If one notices that the dog is subject to colds, one should permit him to sleep in a warm corner in the house during the winter.

Jackets

In cold and wet weather, it is a good idea to put jackets on certain breeds when they are taken out. This is not a question of unnecessary elegance. The little coats and waterproof capes are often necessary. Delicate dogs who are subject to illness need to be protected from the cold of winter. Some breeds or individual dogs may be particularly susceptible to rheumatism. And, finally, old dogs and puppies are less resistant to the dangers of bad weather. For longhaired dogs, large dogs, and Nordic breeds, one need only use a jacket in case of illness or winter clipping. For the majority of dogs who do not use coats, it is necessary to follow one rule carefully: when bringing the dog in from the rain or snow, one must dry him vigorously all over with a rag. For dark-coated dogs, newspaper is excellent for this purpose, because it is so absorbent. For longhaired dogs, one should only dry the legs and underneath parts. The rest of the body is well protected by the coat, and one only risks allowing the water to penetrate down to the skin. The dog will shake himself to get rid of the drops of water lying on his coat. After drying the dog, one should make him run around a bit. This way he will avoid the pains of rheumatism in his old age.

Collars

If the jacket is an occasional item in the dog's life, three other objects are everyday necessities: the collar, the leash, and the muzzle. The collar should first be put on the dog when he is very young. It is better to use a leather collar than a plastic one, and it should be washed every fifteen days. The dog should also get used to a leash when he is very young. Allowing dogs to wander freely in the streets is a source of bother and of danger and is, in fact, against the law in many places. The dog may dig in garbage, start fights, bite, or be stolen. He should therefore be accustomed at the age of two or three months old to wear a collar and a leash. The collar should be fairly loose. Once it is buckled, one should be able to run one's finger around the inside.

Leash

In principle, the leash should be long enough to permit the dog to feel. free, (about 6 feet, or 2 meters, long). As time goes by, one should shorten it to a normal length of 39 to 47 inches (1 m. to 1 m.20 cm.). If on the first outing, the dog seems afraid because of the traffic, it is a good idea to carry him to the desired spot and then to make him walk home on the leash. The idea of returning home will make the puppy so happy that he will endure walking with a leash more willingly.

Muzzle

It is also necessary to accustom the dog to a muzzle, especially for the short periods in which he is allowed to run free. One should give him his first experience with a muzzle at a very young age, putting it on the dog while he is napping. At first, he will try to get rid of it by knocking it against chairs and doors. But after a while, he will get used to it, and will perhaps have a change of heart and go back to sleep. There are several types of muzzles. In muzzles with metal parts, it is very important to see that the dog does not rub them against things and thus injure himself.

Parasites

All dog owners know that sooner or later the dog will get fleas. As with other parasites, he will need help getting rid of them. Parasites are organisms which live on other living beings. They live either in or on the body of their hosts. Fleas, lice, and ticks are external parasites. Flatworms, roundworms, and worms which live in the stomach, esophagus, and intestines are all internal parasites.

Fleas

The most aggressive and widespread parasites that attack dogs are fleas. They are not only a constant torment to the animal, but also a danger, since they carry infectious germs, can cause sores on the dog's skin, and carry worms. The most effective weapon against fleas is cleanliness. When one notices infestation, one should brush the dog vigorously and check the state of his skin.

Inspecting a dog for fleas may be a lot of work if the dog has long hair. Longhaired dogs with fleas will often need lukewarm baths with doses of antiseptic solution prescribed by a veterinarian. After the bath, examine the dog's head very carefully, because the fleas, in order to survive the flood, may, like victims of a shipwreck, seek a dry island. For rough-haired and longhaired dogs, if a flea powder is needed, select one with a pyrethrum base. It is especially good because it is not toxic to the dog.

Since fleas also reproduce in the place the dog lives, it is necessary periodically to disinfect his cushion or corner as well as all cracks around places he habitually spends time. One should not, however, use a disinfectant with too strong a smell, because it can affect the dog's sense of smell, a particular inconvenience in the case of hunting dogs. Dog fleas are rarely attracted to people.

Lice

Less common, but more disagreeable, than fleas are lice, which cause the dog unbearable itching. One must get rid of these unwanted guests as quickly as possible by suitable washes or by special baths given in a salon. It may even be necessary to shear the dog completely.

Ticks

Dogs who live in the country or who, while hunting or vacationing, run in the fields, may be attacked by a parasite the size of a melon seed, a tick. Ticks suck the blood of sheep and dogs. The tick buries his head under the dog's skin and lives on the nourishment from his blood while causing itching and eventually anemia in his host. This parasite is easily found during periodic brushings because his round body remains outside the skin. But it is a grave mistake to pull the tick away without taking precautions. The ticks come away easily, but they leave their heads inside the dog's skin. These decay and cause small annoying infections. In order to detach a tick scientifically, soak a small wad of cotton in alcohol (ether is quite effective too), and place it directly on the tick for several minutes. Then wait a minute or two and remove the tick gently with tweezers, being careful not to break its body and bringing along the head and pincers. A prolonged infestation of ticks may be dangerous, because ticks can carry Rocky Mountain Spotted Fever.

Roundworms

Roundworms, whipworms, and hookworms are the most common intestinal parasites in dogs. Roundworms are cylindrical worms about $1\frac{1}{2}$ to $4\frac{1}{2}$ inches (4 to 11 cm.) in length, similar to those found in man. They may inhabit dogs of any age, but are especially common in puppies. Dogs become infected by licking objects on which the parasite's eggs have been laid. Suckling puppies can be infected directly from the breasts of their mother. These worms reproduce so prolifically that they may form a mass which blocks the intestines. When a dog has worms, he may have any of the following symptoms: a capricious appetite, loss of weight, alternation between diarrhea and constipation, vomiting, anal itching, nervousness, or dull hair. The worms may be emitted spontaneously in the dog's excrement, and in this case, there is no doubt about the diagnosis. It is better, however, to have a veterinarian examine a stool sample under a microscope. He can detect the eggs of the worm and prescribe the proper worming medicine.

Whipworms

Whipworms concentrate in the caecum (a structure similar to the human appendix). Possible symptoms of whipworms are emaciation, nervousness and a watery, bloody stool. The condition requires veterinary treatment.

Hookworms

Ancylostomiasis is a parastic disease caused by hookworms, a worm of the genus Ancylostoma. It is common in hunting dogs. These little worms burrow into the intestinal lining and suck the blood, causing anemia. In these cases, worming is necessary, accompanied by treatment for anemia. English breeders advise worming puppies once every two months and adult dogs once a year. Nevertheless, it is a good idea to consult a veterinarian in whom you have confidence about worming.

Tapeworms

The tapeworm is another common parasite found in the dog's intestines. The infested animal may have no symptoms, but more often, he will have diarrhea alternating with constipation and a voracious appetite combined with loss of weight. Sometimes, dogs with tapeworms become nervous or are even subject to seizures. One can be sure that the dog has a tapeworm when small, ricelike segments of worm appear in his stool. Treatment consists of administering the proper dosage of worming medicine.

Itching

If it is not caused by parasites, itching is usually the result of some other illness, ordinarily a skin disorder. It may, however, also be a symptom of diabetes, chronic nephritis, or digestive disorders. Autointoxication and poor diet may also cause itching in dogs. The way to deal with itching is to diagnose and treat the cause. While waiting to see the veterinarian, one can relieve the dog's discomfort with various sprays, cold water, and alcohol or camphor rubs. In any case, it is a good idea to feed the dog a diet of rice and vegetables for several days.

Mange

One skin disorder which causes itching is mange. It especially attacks young dogs. It requires isolation and can only be treated by a veterinarian.

Education

Two elements should act as stimulants in the education of a young dog: reward and punishment. The reward may be an affectionate word, a pat, a compliment, or a goody. The punishment should be a reproach given in a strong tone of voice, a tap on the back with a rolled-up newspaper, or a light tap with the hand. When the puppy enters the house for the first time, he should be shown his sleeping place and told to "lie down" in a clear, sweet voice. In time, he will learn to obey at a word and will retire immediately when his master wishes.

The puppy needs six outings a day, which may later be reduced to four. It is a good idea to standardize the time of his walks, for example at 8 A.M., 10 A.M., 12:30 P.M. (after his meal), 3 P.M., 7 P.M. (after his second meal), and 11 P.M. If the puppy makes a mess in the house, reprimand him in a strong voice while holding his head near the mess and giving him a light spanking. If one then takes care to carry him immediately to the terrace, garden, or street where he may properly take care of his needs, he will soon understand what his master wishes. As soon as the puppy begins to use the desired spot, one should compliment him, pet him, give him a biscuit, and make him understand he has pleased you. When the dog has become used to relieving himself in the street, usually around the fifth to eighth month, the walks for elimination may be cut back, first to five and then to four times a day: around 8 A.M., 12:30 P.M., 7 P.M., and 11 P.M. At least one of these walks should last a half-hour to one hour.

Generally, the dog will be happy to obey his master. At first, he is obliged to obey, then he wishes to obey, taking pleasure in doing what his master wants. There are, however, dogs with difficult and even unmanageable characters, though these are rare. For the obedient dog, it is unnecessary to yell orders; it is enough that they be given in a calm but firm voice. The dog may be taught to obey even a hand gesture.

Relationship with Other Dogs

Dogs get along with man, but often they have little liking for other dogs. Some dogs show themselves to be biters at an early age, and their hostility carries over to horses, cows, chickens, and even mechanical toys. It is therefore necessary to train a dog early by putting him in contact with other dogs and grabbing him by the scruff of the neck at the first sign of naughtiness, while petting him for remaining calm. Teaching an older dog to give up fighting is less easy, since his hostility is ingrained. When faced with a fight between adult dogs, the most effective system of disengaging them is to grab the dog by his hind legs with one hand and hit him with the other until he loosens his hold on the other dog. It is rare that one should have to hit a dog with his leash. It is especially important to watch small dogs, such as Dachshunds and terriers, because they are very courageous and will attack dogs much bigger than themselves.

Name

The dog's name plays a role in the formation of his personality and in his education. It is, therefore, important to accustom the dog to coming when called as early as possible and not wait until he is older. If he is a purebred dog, he probably has a complicated name given him by his breeder as a result of his pedigree. In the house, however, he should be called by a short simple name of one or two syllables, like Bob, Blackie, Flag, or Susy, which will sound to his sensitive hears like a clear command. The puppy will quickly learn that he has a name and that when called, he should come to his master. One should begin to associate his name with pleasant things so that its sound will remind him of a kind word, a treat, a game, or a walk. This is why in the beginning, one should never call a dog by his name when disciplining.

If one follows this advice, it will not be long before the dog will gladly come to his master at the first call. Each time he responds thus, one should give him a pat. It may happen that the dog will not come immediately because he is comfortable and warm in his bed, because he is in the midst of some game, or because he is distracted by something. In these cases one should insist, and then when he does come, reward him with a pat or dog biscuit and a kind word.

In cases where the disobedience persists or in cases of feigned deafness, the best measures to adopt are the following: Put a collar around the puppy's neck and attach a long cord to it. Call the puppy. If he does not come, pull the cord gently, drawing him to you little by little, while calling his name in a calm voice. When he reaches you, pet him as if he had come spontaneously and play with him a little to distract him. The dog must never forget this first elementary lesson in the house and, above all, in the street where the dangers to dogs are becoming greater and greater.

Games

In winter, when sunny days are rare, when it rains and is cold, the dog cannot play outside. He still needs, however, relaxation and movement. Without this, he will become lazy and fat, slow and sad. This is why besides walks for elimination, he must have some exercise in the house and be played with. One must choose appropriate playthings, nothing too small that he might swallow, and nothing sharp that might injure him. The best toys are those made of solid rubber in the shape of bones, cat's heads, or batons. One should not give a dog the kind of balls usually used in children's games, because his sharp teeth will quickly tear them apart. A bit of swallowed rubber can cause serious intestinal disorders.

Training

There is a distinction between education and training. Education which is undertaken by all dog owners means that a one-year-old dog must not mess in the house, must come when called, must not bark when left alone, etc. Training, on the other hand, is undertaken in specialized schools with the goal of obtaining, according to the breed, a watchdog, a guard dog, an attack dog, a herd dog, a truffle dog, a police dog, or a guide for the blind. People who wish to have their dogs trained must send them to special schools for two to eight months where their latent abilities will be developed to their utmost in order to make the dog useful.

Conditioned Reflexes

Conditioned reflexes are extremely useful for educating and training a dog. They consist of a psychological phenomenon of association between a certain stimulus and a certain reaction. The dog has a remarkable associative memory. In a short time, our actions produce corresponding reactions on his part. For example, the sight of his leash will bring to mind the happy prospect of a walk, and the sight of his dish will remind him of the joy of eating.

Reward and Punishment

When the dog understands and executes that which one wishes him to learn, it is important, as has been said, to reward him immediately. Likewise, he must be punished for doing things one considers naughty.

With reward and punishment, one achieves the association of the ideas of pleasure and displeasure, which will help the dog to execute or avoid an action. Though one must not be too harsh in punishing a dog, one must be generous in rewarding him with biscuits, pats, and kind words. The dog wants his master's love and happiness, and for this satisfaction he will obey orders.

Punishment and correction ought to be instant. They must follow immediately upon the dog's misdeed, because after time has passed, he will not understand and will merely become afraid of his master. For some dogs, it is sufficient that the master raise his voice a bit and give a light tap with a rolled-up newspaper, a lot of noise, and little pain. The hand and the leash should rarely be used to punish a dog. With difficult dogs, more severe punishment is necessary, but the harshest punishment with a whip or rod should only be used in the most serious cases, such as when the dog is dangerously aggressive.

Vaccination

Dogs, especially young dogs, are subject to viral attacks. Viruses differ from normal bacteria by being so small that they cannot be differentiated under a microscope and because they multiply like living matter. The most common canine viruses are those that cause distemper, leptospirosis, and viral hepatitis, all illnesses which can be prevented by vaccination. Every dog, purebred or mutt, big or little, city dog or country dog, should be vaccinated against these viruses.

Dogs under two months of age should not have contact with any dogs other than their mothers and siblings. At the age of two months, they should be vaccinated by a veterinarian with a three-way vaccine and kept isolated for two weeks longer so that the immunity can become strong. The veterinarian will give you all the necessary instructions for repeating the vaccinations, which should be given to the adult dog until he is seven or eight years old.

Distemper

Distemper is a dangerous and extremely contagious disease which is known all over the world and which strikes young dogs (never people) between the ages of a few months and one year. Dogs that succeed in recovering from the disease become immune, but they are rare. Distemper is caused by a virus whose damaging activities are aggravated by secondary germs. The onset of the infection is favored by generally debilitating conditions (chills, poor diet, bad breeding) and follows upon direct contact with sick animals or indirect contact with infected materials, such as nasal mucous or saliva coming from the respiratory or digestive tracts, respectively. It may appear as a catarrh, hitting the respiratory and gastrointestinal systems and the conjunctive tissue of the eye; or the dog may break out with pustules; or in its nervous form, the dog may have seizures and cramps.

The dog becomes feverish, has runny eyes, lacks appetite, and sometimes vomits. The diagnosis is usually pessimistic, because the disease, especially if it attacks the nerves, is almost always fatal. Injured nervous tissues have great difficulty regenerating.

The prevention of distemper by vaccination has made great progress and, today, offers a high percentage of immunity. It is necessary to vaccinate the dog once at around three to four months of age and to renew the immunization at intervals prescribed by the veterinarian. Distemper can be treated with antibiotics, with injections to stimulate the liver, and with medications specifically directed toward combating the virus in different parts of the body.

Chorea, or Saint Vitus' Dance

Chorea, or Saint Vitus' dance, may come as a sequel to distemper. It is characterized by the repeated and rhythmic contractions of certain groups of muscles. Chorea may be serious and run a progressive course or be less serious and chronic. It locates itself in one spot in the body (legs, trunk, face) and the rhythmic contractions persist like a tic, even during sleep. Sometimes the symptoms get better with the years, but it is rare that the trouble disappears totally. The treatment, always under the control of a veterinarian, consists of using sedatives and fortifying tonics to improve the dog's health, a good diet, and fresh air.

Leptospirosis

The second infectious illness which usually causes death in dogs is leptospirosis. The prognosis is only optimistic if the disease is caught in its earliest stages. As had been said, one must watch out for and vaccinate the puppy. Leptospirosis is caused by spirochete germs which are found in the urine and feces of sick animals. It is thus that a dog may be infected. There is also an icterohaemorrhagic form of the disease which may be transmitted to the dog by rats. Immediate intervention by a veterinarian is essential.

Viral Hepatitis

The third serious illness in dogs is viral hepatitis. It, too, is preventable by vaccination. It appears like jaundice, because the whites of the eyes and the mucous membranes turn yellow. The dog will be very restrained and will not eat. One must call the veterinarian immediately.

Rabies

Rabies is rare nowadays and has disappeared in many civilized countries. But it is necessary to discuss it since it is one of the few diseases that can be passed from dog to man and since cases still crop up in the United States. It is passed when an infected dog bites a man, and if there is not immediate medical intervention, the result is usually fatal. Rabies cannot appear spontaneously; it is always gotten by contagion. In order to avoid the disease, a bitten person must undergo vaccination, taking advantage of the long period of incubation, which may last up to three months. After the period of incubation, the disease will show up, sometimes violently, sometimes less so. The dog's usual mood will change. He will pass from periods of extreme agitation to depression. He will avoid the light, hide in isolated spots, and become irritable. Sometimes, his voice will become hoarse or he will break into howling. Salivation will become heavy and swallowing food or water will become painful (because of edema of the glottis). After the first stage of the illness, the dog will become violent, biting objects, animals, and people. Finally, he will be seized by paralysis and die in a few days. If a dog with rabies has not bitten anyone, he must be destroyed. If he bites people, he must be put under observation to be sure he really does have rabies. If he does not die in fifteen days, it is not a case of rabies. If he does die, one can be sure it is rabies, and taking into account the incubation period, bitten people must begin the process of vaccination in order to be saved. Since a vaccine is available, it is silly to run the risk, however small, of your dog contracting rabies.

Winter

Healthy dogs love snow. One should therefore let them run and play in the snow, for up to an hour if the dog is a city dog and as long as half a day if he is a country or mountain dog. Once he comes back inside, he should be carefully dried. Here is some practical advice for a dog in winter:

1 Watch out for drafts and chills. On the other hand, do not allow the dog to sleep beside a radiator.
2 One should not put a jacket on a dog unless he is very old or young, weak, or a miniature or shorthaired breed, or convalescing from an illness. Mature, healthy, longhaired dogs have been given a thick coat by nature, and this affords complete protection.
3 Don't worry about rain or snow. The only precaution one need take, as has been suggested so often, is to dry the dog thoroughly on his return, especially his legs and chest. He will get rid of the excess moisture in his coat himself by shaking.
4 If he jumps into the water by himself, let him. Dogs who like to swim in all weather are usually healthy and strong. When he comes out, dry him thoroughly and make him take a long run.
5 Do not feed him food that is too cold or give him ice water. Everything should be room temperature.
6 If the dog is healthy and has a thick coat, leave him outside even if it is cold, but not if it is raining hard or is very windy. Avoid, as

much as possible, abrupt changes from hot to cold and vice versa.

7 Baths at home or in a salon should be given regularly even in winter. Dry the dog carefully with an electric hair dryer.

8 When riding in a car, the dog should not sit by the door, as he can catch cold or an inflammation of the respiratory tract, the eyes, or the ears.

9 If the dog becomes ill, let him rest in a room with a constant temperature. The veterinarian will give the necessary instructions to keep the sickness from becoming serious.

10 Always keep a little winter pharmacy in the house: boric acid for warm eye-compresses, aspirin for colds (a half-tablet in some warm milk), essence of turpentine for inhalations in cases of colds with respiratory problems (three drops in a small bowl of boiling water; hold the animal near enough to breathe the vapors for several minutes).

Colds are not the only danger to a dog in winter. He may also be subject to frostbite and chills. Localized frostbite (on the feet) is a common condition, especially with mountain dogs. One should treat it by rubbing the affected part with snow or cold water, then wrapping it in wool. Or one can soak the leg in lukewarm water to which one gradually adds hot water until it reaches about 94.5° to 103.5° F. (35° to 40° C.). When the foot regains its feeling, smear it with lukewarm oil.

Spring

For most dogs, the cold season is one long indoor rest, and he does not really go out until spring. It is important to help him cast off his winter lethargy. Spring is a good time for long walks, for cleaning him carefully, and for varying his diet.

On a sunny day, one should clean the dog's bed thoroughly, throwing out his old mattress. Everything should be aired, washed, and disinfected. In spring, the dog should be bathed more often, and he should be brushed every day with a hard scrub-brush. If one owns a dog of a breed that should be clipped, the end of April or May is a good time to take care of this. It is a good idea to add to the quantity of green vegetables and meat in the dog's diet, adding at the same time a small spoonful of olive oil. Some hygienists recommend giving the dog a pinch of Epsom salts dissolved in lukewarm water every morning for ten days early in spring. The solution should be poured into the side of the dog's mouth to make him swallow it. Even if your dog is in good health, he should be taken to the veterinarian for a checkup.

Warm Weather

Dogs do not sweat. Nevertheless, the skin eliminates wastes by means of the sebaceous glands. The sudoriferous glands are inactive or even nonexistent. Dogs supplement their deficient perspiration, so necessary for health, by increased kidney activity and by panting. When the dog is tired or overheated, he breathes more quickly. By drawing in a great quantity of air, he is able to lower the temperature of his blood as it reaches his lungs, refreshing his body in much the same way as would be achieved by sweating. One should not leave a dog tied up in the sun or in a warm spot for too long.

Heatstroke and Sunstroke

The warm season exposes the dog to two dangers which have identical symptoms: heatstroke and sunstroke. It often happens that the master does not have the consideration he ought to for his dog and leaves him in a car in the sun, on the hot sand of the beach, sets him to work in the sun without sufficient water, forgets him on the balcony during the hottest part of the day, or takes him for long walks in the mountains with rests in the sun without having thought to bring a bottle of water and a bowl with him. In all these cases, the dog is threatened with succumbing to heatstroke or sunstroke. The first sign of sun- or heatstroke will be that the dog will begin to pant violently. His breathing will accelerate, his eyes will protrude, his tongue will become bluish purple, his step will become uncertain, and he will finally fall to the ground. In such a dramatic situation, the first thing to do is call the veterinarian, because the dog may have only two or three hours to live. While waiting for medical aid, the owner may take some steps on his own. Take off the dog's collar and muzzle. Carry him to a cool, shady spot, not allowing him to exert himself. Put cold compresses on his head and body. It is also advisable to give him a small spoonful of coffee to stimulate his heart. In order to calm him, the master should speak to him in a low voice and pet him. The veterinarian will give him an injection to restore the tone to his organism.

Summer

At the beginning of summer, the dog has need of special care. Here are ten recommendations for helping your dog have a pleasant summer:

1 See that the dog is clipped or stripped if he belongs to one of the following breeds: Poodle, Wire Terrier, Scottish Terrier, Airedale, Schnauzer, Griffon, and similar breeds. One should never clip the following: German Shepherd, Collie, Spitz, Maltese, Pekingese, Cocker, Setter, etc. Their coats thin themselves in hot weather.
2 In the house, let him choose the place where he wishes to sleep. If he suffers greatly from the heat, let him rest in a dim or dark room.
3 A bowl of water, refilled two or three times a day, should always be kept available to the dog in a corner of the kitchen. When traveling, never forget to bring along a thermos or bottle of tap water and a bowl so that you may give the dog a drink.
4 In his meals, give the dog cooked, rather than raw, meat mixed with rice and vegetable broth. When traveling, it will be more convenient to feed the dog enriched dog biscuits and packaged dog food.
5 When traveling, the dog should not sit next to the door of the car. The air can give him conjunctivitis, otitis, or sore throat. If the dog is left alone in the car, be sure and park in a shady spot.
6 In the country, let the dog run in fields where there are no sheep, chickens, or cows. Never allow him to run free in no-hunting zones; he might be shot by the game warden.
7 Before taking your dog to the beach, find out about all restrictions. In any case, it is a good idea to inform the proprietor of the beach of his presence and then to tie the dog up under an umbrella to avoid his relieving himself or bothering others. Swimming in the sea is healthy for a dog, but should be avoided with pregnant bitches or bitches in heat.
8 If one wishes to bring a dog into a hotel, it is good to warn the proprietors in advance. In general, dogs are not allowed to eat in the bedrooms, but must be fed in a back room or bathroom. Dogs in hotels must not bark.
9 On train trips, dogs must travel in the baggage car in portable kennels. Only Seeing Eye dogs may travel in passenger cars. Therefore, it is important to be sure your train has a baggage car and that both your departure and arrival station accept checked baggage.
10 If one does not wish to take the dog along on a vacation, one should reserve a place early in a good kennel.

Dogs and Small Children

Dogs and small children are usually great friends and get along well, especially when they are used to living together from infancy. Dogs generally show great patience with children; however, old dogs are less interested in making new friends and may become angry if a little child jumps on them or steps on their tails.

Jealousy

It often happens that a child is born into a house in which a dog has lived for some time. One of the most obvious reactions for the dog may be jealousy. Whether the dog appears jealous or, on the contrary, seems overaffectionate toward the baby, it is a good idea to be sure not to leave him alone in the room with the crib. One should not, however, chase him away brutally, for this may turn his otherwise amicable feelings for the child into resentment. It is unusual for the incompatibility between the dog and the baby to be great enough to make it necessary to give the dog away. Usually, the dog will adapt during the first weeks, and by the time the child can walk, peace will have been made. This is especially true if the child does not tease or play too roughly with the dog. The relationship will probably be an affectionate one, and it is a good idea to see that this does not go too far, even if the dog is healthy and clean. One should avoid the dog licking the child or the child kissing the dog, and such hygienic measures as baths and use of disinfectants should be stepped up. One occasionally hears talk about diseases such as echinococciasis and rabies, which dogs may give to people and especially to little children. But one should not be overly concerned about this. The former is a disease which is only transmitted by dogs living in the country in close association with sheep or dogs fed on the viscera of such animals. The latter has become extremely rare and can only be transmitted by wild dogs or cats who are already contaminated.

It is always good to teach children how to behave with the dog and vice versa. Children should learn that a dog is not a mechanical toy, but a living being who should not be disturbed while he eats or teased while he sleeps. They should be taught not to hug him to the point of suffocation, not to allow him to lick them on the hands or face, and not to share food or drink with him. As for the dog, he should be trained to watch out for the children and to be careful of his own strength in their games. A large and active dog can easily injure or knock down a child. It is better if children not pet dogs they do not know, and it is always important to follow the elementary rules of hygiene. Finally, one must teach the child not to bother an expectant bitch or one that has just had her puppies. As the children grow older, they should be taught to help take care of the dog. They may be given the responsibility of feeding him, changing his water, straightening his bed, and taking him for a walk.

Law and Taxes

Dogs are today so much a part of man's life that they, too, are subject to laws and taxes.

In the United States, these regulations are usually determined by and valid throughout the state, except in large cities where local laws prevail.

Laws usually require that a dog be kept on a leash. In general, owners or guardians are responsible for damage caused by their dogs. Hunting dogs and herd dogs are subject to their own regulations, and in the country, there are laws prohibiting dogs from chasing deer and other wild animals. Taxes usually take the form of licensing fees.

Other laws protect the dogs themselves from being stolen, mistreated, or killed.

Train Trips

Dogs are not allowed in passenger cars of most trains in the United States. Instead, they must travel in sturdy portable kennels in the baggage car. In general, they must ride on the same train with an accompanying adult who is going to the same destination. It is important to be sure that the train you wish to take has a baggage car and that both the station of departure and the station at your destination handle checked baggage.

You may visit your dog at any station stop of ten minutes or more and may even take him for a walk if there is time. It is the owner's responsibility to bring enough food for the entire trip. Train personnel will see to it that the dog has plenty of water.

First-class passengers are not charged for an accompanying dog. Coach passengers are charged a fee based on the combined weight of dog and kennel.

Some dogs travel easily. Others, however, adjust poorly to the strain and take a long time to recover from a trip. It is a good idea to consult a veterinarian about your dog's ability to cope with train travel.

Airplane Trips

Large dogs may travel by plane, provided they are in special cases and are registered as baggage. Like baggage, they are paid for by weight. Little dogs, on the other hand, may be carried by their masters as long as there are no other dogs on the same flight. This privilege must be reserved in advance through your ticket agent. Of course, the captain's permission is required. A health certificate stating that the dog has a current rabies shot is almost always required.

Boat Trips

On a boat, a dog is kept in a special cage, with little freedom of movement. He may not enter any of the salons, the bar, or the cabins, but may be walked with a leash on the deck at any hour. The cost varies according to the length of the trip and from one boat to another. Any steamship company or travel agent can give you ample information.

Taxi Rides

Taxis may pose a problem for dogs. Drivers may not permit the dog in their cabs. When, as is most usual, they do, one should keep the dog on one's lap rather than putting him on the seat.

Automobile Trips

Dogs are glad to ride in cars with their masters. They jump in gladly and take their places on the seats with their noses pressed against the windows. It is said that a dog is the best anti-theft device. Whether he is a biter or friendly, his very presence discourages evil-doers.

In cases of long trips, do not forget to stop every 95 to 125 miles (150 to 200 km.) to allow the dog a little walk (always with a leash) by the side of the road. When the car has stopped, accustom the dog to wait for a command before getting out.

If the dog gets carsick, it will be necessary to give him a sedative. The veterinarian will prescribe the proper dosage, depending on the dog's size. In general, it will be half the human dosage. Skipping his breakfast is also a good idea, to avoid bother during the trip. Finally, leaving a window half-open will give him some comfort on hot days.

Kennels

When one is obliged to leave the dog in the city and it is not possible to leave him with someone you can depend on, the best idea is to leave him in a good kennel. Get information from breeders, veterinarians, and the A.S.P.C.A. about the best kennels in your area. Then go and see for yourself how the dogs are housed, fed, and taken care of. Kennels recommended by friends who have already tried them are to be preferred as are those situated in woody hills or fields. They should have large covered sheds, solidly constructed compartments for the dogs, adequate hygienic facilities, a floor of packed earth or ceramic tile, and sufficient personnel to care for the dogs.

At the Hotel with His Master

There are few hotels that will not accept a guest accompanied by a well-trained dog. Some hotels have established a fee for dogs which includes their meals. Some proprietors allow dogs in the dining room, while others prefer that they be fed in the room or in the office. The dog may eat and sleep in the bathroom of one's room, and remain there when his master goes out. Many restaurants have dishes especially for feeding and watering the dogs of their clientele. If the dog is well trained, he will obviously not bark, get up on the beds, sleep on the chairs, eliminate in the room, or growl at the service personnel. If he is allowed in the dining room, the dog must be attached with a leash to his master's chair and must remain quiet so that he does not disturb the other diners. All in all, his presence should hardly be noticed. Hotels and tourist resorts where dogs are not welcome usually advertise this fact on large signs. The picture of a dog with a red cross over him means our friend may not enter.

Quarantine

Many dogs traveling to foreign countries may find themselves compelled to submit to quarantine. This is an unpleasant measure and is probably no longer necessary. It is imposed by such countries as England, Ireland, Denmark, and the United States, where rabies, whose spread it was designed to stop, has long been vanquished. Since the incubation period for rabies is long, there is absolutely no way for a dog traveling from, for example, Italy, and wishing to enter one of the countries where isolation is required to avoid quarantine. The quarantine kennels are usually comfortable, but the excessive period of separation of the dog from his master is not good, especially for small companion dogs.

Sicknesses

While following a dog from birth through his development to the point where he begins the work for which he is trained, we must not forget that he needs our help and consolation. Here, therefore, are illnesses which the dog can easily catch, along with brief advice on emergency measures that can be performed when necessary, while waiting for the veterinarian. Dogs are subject to illnesses of the eyes, the mouth, the ears, the respiratory tract, the skin, the digestive tract, the heart, the kidneys, and the legs, just like humans or any other living being.

Diseases of the Eyes — Conjunctivitis

Let us begin by concentrating on the eye of our friend. There are two major conditions which may affect the eye of the dog: conjunctivitis and cataracts. Conjunctivitis is an inflammation of the conjunctiva, the membrane which covers the underside of the eyelids and the back of the eyeball. There are various possible causes of conjunctivitis—wind, dust, chill, or infection—and it may be acute, chronic, or abscessed. The conjunctive membrane becomes red and painful. The dog will try to scratch it with his paws. Treatment consists of getting out any foreign matter and cleaning and disinfecting the eye with a boric acid solution. If the eyes does not get better within twenty-four hours, it is necessary to call the veterinarian. In the case of abscessed conjunctivitis, sulfonamides and antibiotics should be administered under the supervision of the veterinarian.

Cataracts

Cataracts are one of the most disturbing eye conditions, because they involve the clouding of part or all of the lense. It is, doubtless, a serious condition, but it is one of the most common affecting older dogs. Cataracts are sometimes congenital, existing from birth, but normally, they result from such diverse causes as diabetes, poisoning, contusion, and aging. At first, little spots will appear on the lense, then they will slowly spread until they cover the entire lense, making it opaque. This blurs the vision, which in the end is completely lost. The treatment for this condition is essentially surgical and consists of removing the lense. Even the most successful operation only gives mediocre results in animals, because they cannot wear glasses. However, after such an operation, the dog may regain a good part of his sight and supplement his reduced vision with his sense of smell. Cataract operations must be performed in veterinary clinics by specialists.

Teeth and their Hygiene

Toward the end of his first year, the dog has his complete set of teeth. In order to keep them healthy, they should be cleaned three or four times a week. Here is how: While holding the dog's mouth shut, one lifts a lip and passes a damp brush over the front and back teeth. In place of such hasty cleaning of the back teeth, one can give the dog, from time to time, a spongy bone or an apple to chew on. If cleaning is neglected for too long and the teeth become yellow and encrusted with tartar, it is necessary to take the dog to the veterinarian or his assistant, who will remove the tartar with the proper scrapers. If there is much tartar, it can cause inflammation and bad odors. Putting a drop of lemon juice on the toothbrush will prevent the formation of tartar.

Problems with the Mouth

The dog's teeth should be looked after from the first months of his life. Above all, in smaller breeds, it is important to watch and see that the permanent teeth do not come through before the milk teeth have fallen out (around the fourth or fifth month). If this happens, it is recommended that you have the milk teeth extracted by the veterinarian. Otherwise, there is a risk that, in the future, the animal will have deformations of the mouth that will be difficult to correct.

Cavities

Dogs, above all, in their old age, are subject to cavities which may cause them great pain, difficulty in chewing, lack of appetite, and bad breath. The only treatment is removing the affected tooth. Sometimes there will be some infection at the base of a bad tooth, but disinfectant washes after the tooth has been removed will cure them. In the United States, fillings like those used for people have been attempted. But the results are seldom good, because dogs do not lend themselves easily to the drilling necessary for lasting results.

Inflammation of the Gums

Dogs are also subject to inflammation of the gums. There are various causes of this, but usually it is a result of dirty teeth and is associated with stomatitis. One may try washing the dogs teeth after every meal with a piece of cotton dipped in hot saltwater. In cases of ulceration or dental abscess, the veterinarian will administer antibiotic shots to reduce the inflammation.

Stomatitis

Stomatitis is an inflammation of the mucous membrane of the mouth. It causes reddening of the membranes and the appearance of painful ulcers and may affect the gums, the tongue, and the inside of the cheek. It is caused by external irritants, such as hot liquids or other substances, by tooth decay, or is a secondary sympton of diseases of the digestive tract. This disease will be cured in a few days if the causes are ameliorated and the mouth is rinsed with antiseptic solution. Lemon juice diluted with water is recommended, since it will disinfect the mouth and the intestines. If the animal is depressed, a spoonful of coffee will stimulate his spirits. In the most serious cases, the dog should be fed only liquids.

Pyorrhea

This is a chronic ailment of the dental root system which is common among older dogs. Its first symptom is inflammation of the gums. Then the teeth loosen and fall out. One can try a local treatment consisting of washes of tincture of iodine and glycerine, combined with a general treatment of sulfonamides, antibiotics (if there is pus), and vitamins. If the gum is injured, the veterinarian will have to extract the tooth.

Papilloma

Papilloma is another affliction which may affect a dog's mouth. It is a wartlike growth which begins in the mouth and spreads rapidly to the cheeks. It is a contagious disease, but is easily cured by surgery, cauterization, or drugs.

Bad Breath

This is a common problem with dogs. It may be caused by the first meat-based meals, in which case it will disappear on its own. Otherwise, it may be due to dirty or decayed teeth, gastritis, or malfunctioning of the kidneys. If the trouble persists, take the dog to a veterinarian.

Hearing

The dog has very sensitive hearing. He can recognize the footsteps of his master, the motor of his car, the clink of his leash, a distant bark in the country. Furthermore, he hears sounds inaudible to the human ear, but he suffers from excessively loud or penetrating sounds.

Ear Problems — Otitis

When the dog makes shaking or jerking movements with his head, it almost always means ear problems. The most common affliction is otitis, an acute or chronic inflammation of the outer, middle, or inner ear. External otitis, which affects the outer auditory tract, is common, especially in breeds with long, hanging, hairy ears. It may be caused by foreign objects or, more easily, by the dirt which accumulates in ear wax. The acute form is characterized by pain, inflammation, pussy secretions, and a peculiar smell. Caught in time, it is easily cured. Neglected, it becomes chronic and requires long, patient treatment. It is, therefore, indispensable to take the dog to the veterinarian immediately. Internal otitis is rare in dogs and is generally a complication of external otitis. The symptoms are the same, but more pronounced. Besides the pain, the dog will have a high fever and sometimes vertigo and convulsions. The treatment is a combination of antibiotics and hygiene. Parasitic otitis is caused by a mitelike parasite and is contagious. The symptoms are violent itching, inflammation, and, sometimes, convulsions and epileptic-type fits. Treatment consists of medicated washes of the ear canal and generally cures the condition quickly; but neglected, the condition may lead to deafness.

Deafness

This is also common in old dogs. When one finds out the dog is deaf, one should examine the ear canal minutely to find out the cause of the deafness. The treatment will be decided by the veterinarian, but in cases of congenital deafness, it is difficult to obtain good results.

Diseases of the Respiratory System

Dogs, like people, are subject to chills, colds, bronchitis, and rheumatism. A common cold may be caused by a chill due to a draft, by sudden changes in temperature or humidity, or by rain. Its symptoms are sneezing, runny nose, and an irritation of the nasal membrane which will cause the dog to rub his nose against everything. He may have difficulty breathing, and, in any case, will be listless and lacking in appetite. The cold, or catarrh, will normally last only a few days, but it should not be ignored. In puppies, these symptoms may be the first signs of distemper. Sneezing is a much more serious symptom in dogs than in people. If it lasts a whole day, a veterinarian should be called.

If the nose of a dog who has caught cold shows signs of irritation, it should be bathed gently in lukewarm water, dried, and oiled with olive oil. The sick dog should be kept in a warm room with a constant temperature and protected against drafts. He should be kept on a light diet.

Tonsillitis, Pharyngitis, Laryngitis

Dogs are very susceptible to tonsillitis, which causes difficulties in swallowing and, sometimes, vomiting. Tonsillitis is treated with antibiotics but in cases where the illness recurs frequently, the veterinarian may recommend a tonsillectomy, or removal of the tonsils.

Tonsillitis, pharyngitis, laryngitis, or inflammation of the tonsils, pharynx, or larynx, are among the various disturbances grouped together under the general term "sore throat." They can be treated with sulfonamides and antibiotics in suppository or injection form.

Influenza

The influenza a dog catches is different from the human variety, and it is not contagious to man. It is an infectious disease caused by a so-called filterable virus and is similar to distemper, but much less serious. Canine influenza may appear in three forms: the catarrhal form, which affects the respiratory tract; the abdominal form, which may develop into gastroenteritis; or the bronchopulmonary form.

Bronchitis

Influenza and bronchitis are similar conditions. Bronchitis is an inflammation of the mucous membrane which covers the bronchial tubes. It is common in dogs and is associated with other diseases of the respiratory system such as colds, sore throats, and, sometimes, pneumonia. The symptoms of bronchitis are discomfort, loss of appetite, and a fever of about 101.6° F. (39° C.). At first, the cough is dry, then it becomes phlegmy and is followed by a nasal discharge and difficult breathing. These symptoms disappear slowly until recovery is completed in about ten days. The disease may become chronic, in which case the symptoms will be less intense, but will last longer. Old dogs, and those with asthma or cardiac conditions often have chronic bronchitis, especially in winter.

A dog with bronchitis should be protected from the cold and damp. Expectorants, antiseptic and balsam-based cough medicines, and sedatives given in sweetened warm milk are useful in treatment. Sulfonamides, antibiotics, and small pine suppositories may also be prescribed by a veterinarian. During his sickness, the dog should be given light, easy-to-swallow foods.

Pneumonia

Pneumonia is an inflammation of the lungs caused by various germs, following a cold. It is rare in dogs and usually occurs as a complication of distemper. It may be simple, or double, depending on whether it attacks one lung or two. It may be associated with bronchitis (bronchopneumonia) or with pleurisy (pleuropneumonia). The symptoms are a notable weakness, lack of appetite, high fever of 103.4° to 105°F. (40° to 41°C.), difficulty in breathing, coughing, and nasal discharge. The course of the disease is short, and within a few days, the dog will either recover or die, often due to cardiac complications. Veterinary supervision and antibiotic treatment are indispensable. Pneumonia can also be caused by a foreign substance in the lungs, such as liquid medicine which has been improperly administered.

After pneumonia, convalescence is a long process, which should be closely supervised. The dog should not leave the house for at least a month after he recovers and then should resume his normal life slowly.

Oxygen is administered to dogs with pneumonia, those who have suffered a shock, or those who must have a general anesthetic. If one has an old dog with asthma or cardiac troubles, one should always keep a small container of oxygen in the house.

Asthma

Asthma shows itself by an obvious difficulty in breathing and in frequent coughing fits. In attacks primarily older dogs, especially obese ones or those affected by heart trouble or lung trouble (emphysema). Breathing is difficult when the dog runs even a short way or when he climbs stairs. The sick dog will spread his front feet, breathe loudly, and cough as if to free himself from something caught in his throat. Dogs with asthma can be cured only partially. (The veterinarian will prescribe effective medication.) They need dry air, a limited diet, medical attention, and rest.

Rheumatism

Rheumatism of either the joints or the muscles is common in dogs who are exposed to cold and damp weather or to swampy areas. Even in cases where the rheumatism is caused by infection, chills play an important part. When the pains occur, the dog will groan at the least movement, limp sometimes on one foot and sometimes on the other, and his joints will swell. Usually, the dog will have an acute attack which will subside in about a week if there is no relapse. Chronic rheumatism is less painful but is longer and more bothersome, returning every winter. Treatment for rheumatism is generally local and should be undertaken by a veterinarian.

Tuberculosis

Tuberculosis in dogs has nearly completely disappeared, thanks to pasteurization of milk, and it is rare that a dog can be infected by his sick master, as, for example, by eating his leftovers. At the beginning of the illness the symptoms are mild and pass unnoticed. The animal becomes listless and a little feverish, and then begins to cough. An X ray will determine exactly the severity of the illness. In mild cases, cure may be achieved by antibiotics, a healthy diet, and careful hygiene. But in advanced and severe cases, it is advisable to put the dog down, as the treatment is very long and of doubtful outcome.

Skin Diseases

When a dog licks insistently at one area of his body, it is a sign that either some sort of trouble will soon appear or that the dog has a sore or the beginning of an abscess. One should examine the spot in question, and if it is red, a common remedy is to wash the dog with saltwater. If after this, he continues to lick, one should take him to the veterinarian. Certain breeds, such as Poodles and Cockers, often lick the bottoms of their feet. To stop them, it is enough to cut the hair between their toes.

Erythema

This is the mildest inflammation of the skin and is only a reddening of the surface. It is known as primary erythema when it is due to burns, too much sun or cold, or allergic reactions. It is called secondary erythema when it follows upon other illnesses. The skin becomes red, and itching and pain follow. The trouble may last several hours or several days. Then it will disappear without leaving a trace. Drying powders, sulfa-based ointments, antibiotics, cortisone, and anti-histamines are often used to treat this condition.

Eczema

The most common skin problem in dogs is eczema. It is an inflammation characterized by reddening blistering, and crusting of the skin. Usually, eczema is caused by autointoxication of the intestinal tract. Its symptoms are intense itching, oozing, and lesions caused by scratching. The illness is most frequent in old dogs, and is often tenacious, unpredictable and recurrent. Other causes of eczema may be inadequate hygiene, flea or tick bites, the use of irritating soaps, vitamin deficiency, and allergies. Acute eczemas may clear up in a few days, while more chronic cases are often subject to relapse, especially in summer, in dogs who are old, obese, or prone to skin problems. Treatment, general and local, should be prescribed by a veterinarian after a period of observation. While the dog is ill, he should be fed a diet without meat, based on white fish, vegetables, and some cheese. In case of uncontrollable itching, the dog's feet should be bandaged to prevent him from scratching and wounding himself. Healing ointments should be applied before the dog is walked, so that he will be distracted and not lick them off.

Alopecia, Seborrhea, Acne

The skin and hair of the dog are also subject to other illnesses: alopecia (baldness), seborrhea (excessive oiliness), and acne. This last condition is an inflammation of the sebaceous glands and the hair follicles. It is usually caused by bacteria which penetrate the skin through tiny lesions, such as those caused by the rubbing of the dog muzzle. In general, acne is limited to the skin of the muzzle. One will notice nodules the size of the head of a pin which burst and scab over. Acne is treated by washing with water and neutral soap and application of a mixture of iodine and glycerine in equal quantities. *Local* treatment with antibiotics and sulfonamides is also effective. In more tenacious cases, the veterinarian will prescribe treatment with an autogenous vaccine in either ointment or injection form. When an infection of the sebaceous gland spreads to the surrounding tissue, a boil will develop. This is a thick and painful lump whose core is surrounded by pus. The treatment for boils is surgical.

Allergies

Dogs also suffer from allergies that are hypersensitivities to various substances. They may react with rashes, itching, or sneezing. Allergies, however, are usual in dogs and are most often caused by their diets. In some cases, a simple change of food is sufficient. In others, the veterinarian must determine the cause of the problem.

Constipation

Constipation is difficulty in emptying the bowels. It may be caused by too much meat in the diet, too many sweets, lack of exercise, excessive use of laxatives, prostatitis, ingestion of hair balls. or by a variety of other reasons. It is especially common in apartment dogs and pregnant bitches. The animal will be restless, have little appetite, and will try hard to relieve himself. If this lasts more than two or three days, one should call the veterinarian. Treatment consists of enemas, laxatives, glycerine suppositories for puppies, vegetable soups, olive oil, and

269

increased exercise. Before administering drugs, the cause of the constipation should be ascertained.

Intestinal Blockage

One complication of constipation is intestinal blockage, which prevents the passage of feces. It may be caused by foreign objects, hair balls, parasites, or hardened fecal matter. The blockage may occur without warning. The dog will have violent abdominal pains, and his abdomen will be sore to the touch. He will lose his appetite, be excessively thirsty, and, sometimes, vomit. There is nothing to do but take him to the veterinarian. It is unlikely that there will be spontaneous relief. In milder cases, the dog may be relieved by lubricants (oil or Vaseline) or enemas. But in persistent cases, surgery may be necessary.

Gastroenteritis

Gastritis is an inflammation of the mucous membranes of the stomach. It is characterized by pain, nausea, and vomiting. The veterinarian will prescribe treatment with an autogenous vaccine in either ointment or injection form.

It is frequently associated with enteritis, which is an inflammation of the intestinal wall. Gastroenteritis may be primary or secondary, acute or chronic. The principle causes of the condition are mistakes in feeding, irregularity of meals, problems with chewing, spoiled or indigestible food, food which is too cold or too hot, too many sweets, or colds. When it is the stomach that is primarily affected, the dog will be unable to eat solid or liquid foods and will vomit. When the intestines are most severely affected, he will have diarrhea and fever. The acute form is brief, but it may be fatal. The chronic form has the same symptoms, but with less intensity. It is necessary to let the dog rest and to take away his food, giving him only a few spoonfuls of water and lemon juice, water and tea, or water and camomile from time to time. For young and weak dogs, one can feed spoonfuls of bouillon, rice water, tea, camomile, and coffee. The important thing is to stop the diarrhea and vomiting and to clean the intestines. Once the crisis has passed, the veterinarian will instruct you to resume the dog's natural diet gradually.

Diarrhea

In cases of diarrhea, let the dog rest and take away his food for twenty-four hours. Causes of this condition may be colds, extreme fear, poisoning, and illness of the digestive tract. As a sympton, diarrhea may be a sign of the beginning of distemper or of enteritis. If the diarrhea is accompanied by vomiting, seek the help of a veterinarian immediately.

Heart Ailments

Dogs are very emotional animals and are frequently subject to irregular heartbeat. Only a veterinarian can determine if this is a cardiac problem. A master may suspect that his dog has heart trouble if he has excessive difficulty in breathing or if, during the hunt, he becomes fatigued easily, has trembling muscles, or becomes anxious without reason. There is a great variety of heart ailments: arrhythmia, palpitation, pericarditis, myocarditis, hypertrophy, etc. If an afflicted dog becomes excited, he should be made to rest in a quiet place and fed a diet consisting of milk and chopped meat only. The veterinarian will prescribe bromides. If the dog shows signs of weakness, however, it is necessary to sustain his heart muscles with tonics such as digitalis. Dosages of such tonics are extremely important and must be prescribed by a veterinarian. A few drops of brandy or cognac in a small spoonful of coffee may prove temporarily useful in case of collapse due to cardiac fatigue.

Thrombosis

This is rare in dogs. It is the formation of blood clots in the heart and blood vessels which impedes the flow of blood to the muscles of the area involved. It may thus impair the functioning of muscles and organs. It is important to keep the dog quiet while waiting for the doctor. After a while, the circulation may reestablish itself.

Urination

The proper functioning of the urinary system is important, not only for the illnesses which may attack it, but for the illnesses affecting renewal of the blood. If urination appears abnormal or painful, it is a certain symptom of illness and the owner should be alerted. The emission of urine may be greater than usual or diminished, or it may be painful, involuntary, or may even cease altogether. In such cases, one should take the dog to a veterinarian immediately.

Analysis of the dog's urine will help in proper diagnosis. It has already been said that the dog should be taken for a walk four or five times a day to urinate. It is necessary to see that he does not drink excessively during the night. For this reason, one should take away his water bowl after his last walk in the evening. It is interesting to note that the emission of urine in a male dog is controlled by a cartilage in his penis which, when contracted, allows the urine to flow. This reaction is triggered psychologically by the smells on the street. This is why a male dog lifts his hind leg and urinates briefly and frequently. If a dog's thirst is abnormally great—for example two or three times his usual intake—it is an indication that the kidneys are not performing their function of filtering out poisons from the blood fully. The animal, by drinking a lot of water, is trying to help the kidneys do their work. In this case, the dog should be taken to the veterinarian immediately. The treatment is essentially nutritional: a light diet of white meat, such as rabbit, veal, or lean fish. Another cause of poor functioning can be decaying teeth.

Diabetes

Diabetes is a blood disease whose symptoms include increased urination and an almost pathological thirst. One will also notice listlessness, reduced resistance to fatigue, and loss of weight, despite a growing appetite.

The development of diabetes is slow and takes place over months. The best treatment is nutritional. The dog should be fed lean meats, milk, eggs, and vegetable broths. Sugar, which is usually bad for dogs, should always be plentiful. Besides all this, the diabetic dog should live a well-regulated and hygienic life with plenty of exercise. The traditional medical treatment (insulin) should be conducted under the supervision of a veterinarian.

Vivisection

Insulin is one of the few drugs which was developed with the help of vivisection. The dogs sacrificed at the University of Toronto made a great contribution to humanity. However, thousands and thousands of other useless experiments should be inscribed in the black book of cruelty.

Nephritis

This is an inflammation of the kidneys caused by repeated illness or repeated chills. The onset of this condition is deceptive, but after a few days, in acute cases, there will be fever, vomiting, colic, frequent urination, and weakness. Analysis of the urine will allow the veterinarian to diagnose nephritis. Recovery should take place within twelve days, but the prognosis is guarded. Chronic nephritis may have a long period of development with alternative crises and remissions, and the dog may be threatened with eventual death. A "white" diet which excludes meat and salt is indispensable. It should consist of milk, boiled rice, fresh cheese, and a little liver.

Urinary Stones

Urinary stones form in older dogs especially. They may cause nephritis if they form in the kidneys or chronic cystitis if they form in the bladder. In the first case, the dog will be in pain and will frequently assume a pose as if he wants to urinate. In the second case, he will have trouble emitting urine, and that which he does emit will not be clear.

The presence of urinary stones cannot be determined definitively, however, without an X ray. Only medical treatment can cure the condition, and one must consider the possibility of surgery. The veterinarian will prescribe sedative injections to ease the pain.

Cystitis

This is a common bladder infection which may be acute or chronic. The mucous membrane of the bladder becomes irritated or inflamed by germs which find a favorable terrain for development. Overlong retention of urine, irritating substances ingested by the dog and passed in the urine, bladder stones, or chills may lead to this fertile condition. The sick animal will make a great effort to eliminate and will succeed in passing only a few drops of urine which will be murky and give a strong odor. Cystitis usually lasts several days and then responds to veterinary treatment. If the symptoms persist, it is possible that the condition has become chronic. Medical treatment consists of antibiotics and antiseptics.

Prostatitis

The prostate is a gland which lies between the urethra and the bladder. Prostatitis is an inflammation of the prostate and may be either chronic or acute. It is common in older male dogs and may be due to a variety of causes. Its symptoms are difficulty in urinating and defecating, and it requires a rectal examination by a veterinarian. Surgery to remedy prostatitis is not recommended for dogs. Instead, hormone treatments are preferred.

Leg Problems

A dog's feet should be the object of constant attention. For example, they should be examined after every bath.

It is common to find inflammation of the plantar pads. The dog will have difficulty walking and will limp. In mild cases, cleaning with lukewarm water and soap is sufficient. But in acute cases, compresses of denatured alcohol are recommended. These are also useful in cases of whitlows, but if small abscesses occur, it is necessary to consult a veterinarian.

Bursitis

This is a common inflammation of the elbows and knees, or rather the front and rear joints. One should keep the dog quiet, and the veterinarian will prescribe the necessary baths and compresses.

If the dog cannot wear down his nails by exercise, it is necessary to have them cut periodically by a specialist in a grooming salon. Puppies' nails may be filed down at home.

Fear

Dogs often feel afraid, and the instinct for self-preservation will make him flee that which may hurt him. The most common cases of fear are caused by the sounds of gunshots, by thunder storms, fireworks, very loud noises, entering unknown places, and silence. Fear may be congenital, in which case it will be difficult to overcome once it is acquired. In this case, much patience will achieve the best results. One can overcome the fear of gunshot noises by exposing the dog to them while holding him near and petting him when the guns go off, or, if necessary, giving him a treat. One should proceed in the same way when dealing with any loud noise which bothers the excessively sensitive ear of the dog.

Poisoning

Poisoning is produced by the ingestion of toxic substances, such as rat poison or poisoned bits of meat, fed to the dog out of malevolence. Poisoning shows itself in different ways and can lead the owner to believe that the symptoms are caused by a variety of different illnesses. In general, however, the dog is subject to unquenchable thirst, vomiting, diarrhea, vertigo, and cramps. His muzzle becomes hot, and he may become enraged. The picture is dramatic. There are many different toxic substances, and in each case, it is vital to get to the veterinarian as quickly as possible. There is, however, one emergency measure which one may take at the first suspicion that the dog has swallowed poison. One may induce vomiting by feeding the dog warm water into which has been mixed the beaten whites of two or three eggs. Once the stomach has been emptied in this manner, take the animal to the veterinarian without delay.

Drowning

Dogs are by nature good swimmers, and it is rare that they go under. If the dog does show signs of drowning the first thing to do, once he is out of the water, is to hold his head down to help him get the water out of his mouth and nose. Then one should dry him well and wrap him in a coverlet. If the dog seems to have stopped breathing, one should apply artificial respiration. This is done by pressing lightly and repeatedly on the thorax, while moving the tongue, held in your hand with a handkerchief, up, down, and sideways. When the dog shows signs of life, take him to a veterinarian promptly.

Wounds

The different kinds of wounds which a dog, especially a hunting dog, may get may be divided into the following categories:

1 Cuts: Cuts have clean sides and usually bleed. The bleeding should be stopped with bandages. If a large blood vessel has been cut, it is necessary that the veterinarian apply a tourniquet promptly. If a limb has been severed, it is necessary to stop the flow of blood by applying a tight tourniquet above the wound, and to call the veterinarian immediately. Once the bleeding has been stopped, the hair around the wound should be shaved, the wound should be disinfected, and in order to aid in healing, the cut should be stitched. If the dog chews on the sutures, he will cause a sore that will be slow to heal. The sutures are usually removed within a week.
2 Gunshot wounds: These are common in hunting dogs. Wounds caused by bullets are more serious than those caused by bird shot. It is necessary to extract the foreign body, stop the bleeding, and disinfect the wound.
3 Bites: Caused by other dogs, these may be more or less serious and should be treated like other wounds.
4 Poisonous bites: Some bites are caused by bees, wasps, hornets, spiders, or scorpions. The venom of these insects produces, without great pain, a swelling which will disappear in a short time. But there are a number of bites which may lead to grave illness or even death. Fish ointments, paintings of ammonia, and antihistamines are useful against the pain of such bites.

Fractures

Even a dog can "break a leg." The break may be closed, without visible lesion to the skin, or open, with the bone sticking out of the wound. It may be complete, if the bone is totally broken, or partial, if the bone is only cracked. The animal will hold the leg up or hanging and will not be able to put weight on it. In young dogs, simple fractures heal easily, but it is always necessary to immobilize the limp in a cast. Fractures of the spinal column, however, are incurable.

Temperature

Normal temperature for a dog is between 100.2° and 101.3° F. (38.2° to 38.8° C.). It is a little higher in puppies. One should measure the dog's temperature with a mercury thermometer gently placed in the dog's rectum, while the animal is being held firmly by another member of the family. In order to slip the thermometer in more easily, one may put Vaseline on the end. If the temperature is up to 102.5° F. (39.5° C.), it is an indication of illness.

Oral Medication

All medication to be given by mouth, with the exception of medicines which can be dissolved in the dog's food, should be administered as follows: Lift one lip of the animal, right or left, and pour the medication from a spoon into the little pouch formed between the lip and the lower teeth. This way the dog will swallow the medicine even if it tastes bad, without being able to reject it. It is dangerous to force the dog's mouth open and pour a dose of the medicine down his throat.

This may cause suffocation, or in puppies, a form of pneumonia which is almost always fatal.

One may make the dog swallow pills by hiding them in his food, or directly, by opening the dog's mouth, putting the pill at the back of his tongue, and holding his mouth closed until he swallows. This way he cannot spit out the pill. Drops or powders may be mixed with milk.

Length of Life

We have followed the dog since the day of his birth, watching over his education, protecting his health. And now the friend that has given his master so much joy is getting old. We must care for him and be close to him now, even more than when he was strong and alert. Even as his period of gestation is brief, so unfortunately, his life runs its course quickly too. It is said that each year of a dog's life corresponds to seven years of the life of a man, in which case, a two-year-old dog is like a fourteen-year-old child, and an eight-year-old dog is like a man of fifty. But the validity of this simile is only general, because dogs begin to walk after a few days, and they are able to procreate after only nine months, while in man these stages come much later.

A dog usually lives twelve to fourteen years and, occasionally, even fifteen, although there are those exceptional cases of dogs reaching twenty years of age. The dog is in his prime at about three to five years of age. Physically, he is completely developed at that time, his vigor is at its height, and his intelligence at its most lively. At around seven or eight years the dog begins to decline gradually. At this age, a companion dog will seek tranquility, preferring to sleep and valuing a warm corner in winter. Guard dogs and hunting dogs will no longer have the resistance and aggressiveness of their youth. They will begin to gain weight, and white spots will appear in their coats. Their sight and hearing will be less acute, and their bodily functions will not be regular.

As far as the good health of an aging dog is concerned, the way in which he should have been cared for and treated in his youth — sunshine, fresh air, exercise, cleanliness, proper nourishment, protection from the cold, checkups by the veterinarian — should all be continued in his old age.

To keep an aging dog in good shape, it is necessary, in addition to the ordinary rules of hygiene, regular meals, and an ordered life of exercise and rest, to give the dog only moderate amounts of food, see that he lives in a healthy atmosphere, and augment his resistance against infectious germs. One should let him rest and give him easily digested food, with more broth and less meat, so that he does not get fat. One should exercise him, but without exertion.

Dogs usually die peacefully without knowing what is happening. But sometimes, because of incurable illnesses and pain, it is necessary to put them down. Death, in this case, is brought about by an intervenous injection which first puts the dog to sleep, and then stops the beating of his heart. Once again, this is the province of a veterinarian.

In big cities, there are municipal crematoriums for dead dogs. The dog is picked up at his home and one pays a modest fee. In the country, the owner can bury his lost companion in a grave which should be six feet (1 m.) deep. There are even cemeteries for dogs. His death is the only sadness that the dog will cause his master, and it is not his fault.

Alphabetical Index of Breeds

Alphabetical Index of Breeds